A
WHO'S WHO
OF
NICKNAMES

A

WHO'S WHO
OF
NICKNAMES

NIGEL REES & VERNON NOBLE

London
GEORGE ALLEN & UNWIN
Boston　　　　　Sydney

George Allen & Unwin (Publishers) Ltd,
40 Museum Street, London WC1A 1LU, UK

George Allen & Unwin (Publishers) Ltd,
Park Lane, Hemel Hempstead, Herts HP2 4TE, UK

George Allen & Unwin Australia Pty Ltd,
8 Napier Street, North Sydney, NSW 2060, Australia

First published in 1985

British Library Cataloguing in Publication Data

Rees, Nigel
    A who's who of nicknames.
1. Anonyms and pseudonyms   2. Nicknames
I. Title   II. Noble, Vernon
929.4'0216   Z1041
ISBN 0-04-827113-6

Set in 11 on 12 point Palatino by A. J. Latham Ltd
and printed in Great Britain by Thetford Press Ltd, Thetford, Norfolk.

CONTENTS

PREFACE

Nicknaming, which began as a means of identification, has developed into a fascinating branch of linguistics, embracing character assessment and assassination. It combines physical description and achievement, employs humour and ingenuity, and contributes to history, etymology and the gaiety of nations.

A nickname in its simplest and dictionary-defined form is an 'added' name, derived from the Old English word *ecan*, to increase, and becoming an *ekename* (slurred to *nekename*). It has a long history. It preceded surnames; in fact, it provided many a surname when indications of relationships in small communities had run out (such as Robin's son, Dicken's son, Meg's son) and descriptions of work or appearance came in useful — from Fletcher the arrow-maker and Walker (who trampled damp woollen cloth to thicken and strengthen it before the days of machinery) to Cudlip and Redhead, Broadhead and Whitehead, Little and Sturdy.

The Welsh preserved this method longer than most, especially useful when so many families shared the same name, so that they invented **Jones the Post** to distinguish him from **Jones the Milk,** and such a slyly affectionate epithet as **Hallelujah Evans** (loud in chapel). Recently we were told of a window-cleaner called Davis in South Wales who was distinguished by the name **Chamois Davis Jnr.**

In higher circles, without fear or favour, there were such dignitaries as **Eric Bloodaxe** and **Ivar the Boneless**, Viking leaders; a king of the West Franks known as **Charles the Fat,** and an earlier Charles called **Baldhead** *(le Chauve);* a tenth-century ancestor of the Counts of Boulogne known as **Long-nose,** and a Prince of Orange named **Hooknose;** while our famous **William the Conqueror** also had the unflattering nickname of **William the Bastard** because of the liaison between his father, Robert (the Devil), Duke of Normandy, and a tanner's daughter from Falaise. The great Russian family of Tolstoy owes its patronymic to an ancestor who was a servant of **Prince Vasily the Blind** who teasingly gave him this nickname which in Russian means **the Fat One.**

Then there are the honorifics, a vast panegyric of them, encapsulating a whole lifetime in one word — **Good Queen Bess; Albert the Good** (Victoria's consort); **Charles the Wise** (a French King), and a Spanish Charles known as the **Desired**; Alfonso V of Aragon, **the Magnanimous;** Lorenzo, Duke of Florence, one of the Medicis, called **the Magnificent**; and Thomas Aquinas, **the Angelic Doctor**. Then there are all the 'Greats', from English Alfred to Russian Peter; and 'Fathers' galore — all honourably earned nicknames but far too many to be listed comprehensively in this book.

Similarly we have only dipped a toe in the pool of promotional tags which may also be considered as nicknames — the 'First Ladies' of this and that, the 'Kings' of popular music and sport. Popular journalism creates new examples of these labels every day of the week.

What we have done is to concentrate on personalities, individuals who have merited a nickname through some incident in their lives, some quirk or characteristic, attainment or failure, bestowed with gratitude or with malice aforethought. We have also dealt with nicknames given to certain groups of people. Such a collection is bound to be selective, the subject is widespread, and we have ventured to extend it only to include those inanimate objects to which a personal name has been transferred, a class that might be called eponymous nicknames — **Anthony Eden, bloomers, Oscar, bowler, cardigan** are examples. The choice begins far back into history and progresses to the present decade, and new items are continually cropping up.

One of the great attractions of nicknames is that they are not respecters of persons when they get beyond honorifics: kings, presidents and politicians, clergy and gangsters, sportsmen and pop stars — all are in the rogues' gallery, warts and all, often enriching the language and embellishing social history.

Where do they come from? Many from journalists, others from the subjects' 'friends'; some from the family; some from that mysterious anonymity, public opinion, which finds a voice in pubs and clubs and any community get-together.

And we mustn't forget the schoolroom and playground where some of the best — and the cruellest — nicknames abound, and their recipients often carry them right through life. **Four-eyes** for a boy wearing glasses is bad enough, but **Fat-arse** is worse, and a teacher with a squint must be prepared to endure **Cross-eye** or **Kerb-drill** (the road code of 'Look right, look left, then cross'). A boy called Cockroft who boasted of his sexual prowess was known in class as **Cock-aloft**; a tall boy as **Totem Pole**; and a well-developed girl as **Buffers** or **Bouncers** or **Titty Tart**. These are in addition, of course, to the traditional descriptives of **Tubby, Billy Bunter, Lefty, Fatty, Skinny,** and so on. And there are comic inventions such as **Jumper** for someone named Cross (jump across), **Space-age** for the surname Sage, and **Jetlag** for a sleepy individual. What names may the new computer language produce? **Mr Chips** will no longer be a beloved old schoolmaster but a young computer genius.

Then there are the family nicknames, most not escaping from the intimacy of the home or a circle of friends, some becoming public property, such as **Harty-Tarty** for a Duke of Devonshire and **Canis** for another because of his fondness for dogs. Lord Snowdon, the photographer who married Princess Margaret, became known around Buckingham Palace as **Snapshots.**

In places of work, nicknames are rife as people try to come to terms with the peccadilloes and other notable features of their colleagues. A civil servant told us how she dealt with the fact that her room-mate was fat. She referred to her as **the Wedding Cake** or, alternatively, as the **MOF** ('Mound of Flesh'). At other times, a nickname arises from an inevitable desire to play with words. A Chinese salesman called Yip who provided the word-processor upon which this book has been composed was inevitably dubbed **the Micro-Yip**.

A large category has the title 'Inseparables', those inevitably linked with a surname, a genealogy that is losing its popularity. The reason for most is obvious — **Bunch** (of) Keyes, **Blacky** Smith, **Chalky** White, **Doughy** Baker, **Dusty** Miller, **Dusty** Rhodes, **Dicky** Bird, **Muddy** Waters, **Norman** Conquest, **Rabbit** Hutchinson, **Sandy** Brown, **Shiner** Bright and **Shiner** White (both a parody of 'shine a light'), **Shoey** Smith, **Snip** Taylor, **Stitch** Taylor, **Spider** Webb, **Sugar** Cain,

Timber Wood. Some need a little explanation. **Tod** Hunter, for example. It most likely means 'fox hunter', as 'tod' is an obsolete word for fox, based on a word meaning 'bushy' which the Vikings probably brought over. Eric Partridge, however, gave the credit to a certain Isaac Todhunter whose mathematics textbook was familiar to schoolboys in the latter half of Victoria's reign. (At one time Sloans were nick-named Tod out of respect for a famous jockey called Tod Sloan, just as all Peaces were **Charlies**, after Charles Peace, a notorious murderer, and many a Kelly was **Ned** because the exploits of the Australian outlaw became well known.) Every Clarke was once a **Nobby** in deference to the clerks whose dress and status were a cut above the rest — one of the 'nobs' whom we now call 'white collar workers'. Walker is **Johnny** after the brand of whisky, and **Blanco** White com-memorates the trade name of a belt and boot whitener; while **Soapy** Hudson or **Soapy** Pears also refers to a firm's product. **Spud** Murphy reminds us that the Irish at one time were thought to live mainly on potatoes, and **Pedlar** Palmer takes us far back into history when pilgrims back from the Holy Land carried a palm-branch and hawked their way around the country.

Old nicknames can take on new identifications. Places are outside the scope of this book, but Aberdeen, **the Granite City**, has become **Oil City** since the development of the North Sea oilfield of which it has become a supply port; and Rome is no longer the only **Holy City** (of Christendom) now that Manchester has been given the nickname because of the collapse of nineteenth-century sewers, making thousands of holes in the streets, one of which was large enough for a bus to fall in; its old name of **Cottonopolis** is almost forgotten with the decline of the textile industry. Who nowadays would call Edinburgh **the Athens of the North**? Surely not the Greeks who must hesitate before thinking of Athens as the Edinburgh of the South.

We have set ourselves limits and then we have allowed ourselves occasionally to stray beyond them. All we can hope to do is show the exuberant range of nicknames con-cerned with people, describe how they came to be applied, and celebrate the inventiveness and humour they display. We have also shrunk from making judgements on the degree of use to which particular nicknames have been put. Some of the nicknames we record may have attached themselves to people throughout their lives – and beyond. Others may simply be apt coinages, aired but once.

Hazlitt said: 'A nickname is the heaviest stone that the devil can throw at a man' – though, in fact, he was referring more to political labels than personal nicknames. Even so, let the stoning commence.

NIGEL REES
VERNON NOBLE

ACKNOWLEDGEMENTS

We are grateful to the authors and publishers of the following books – in addition to those cited in the text:

Marnham, Patrick, *The Private Eye Story: the First 21 Years* (André Deutsch, 1982).
Miller, Compton, *Who's Really Who* (Blond & Briggs, 1983).
Noble, Vernon, *Nicknames* (Hamish Hamilton, 1976).
Shankle, George Earlie Shankle, *American Nicknames* (The H. W. Wilson Co., 1937).
Sharp, Harold S. (comp.), *Handbook of Pseudonyms and Personal Nicknames* (The Scarecrow Press Inc., 1972/75/82).

A

Abigail: a lady's maid — once-familiar nickname (especially in the days of family Bible reading) derived from the story in 1 *Samuel*, 25. Abigail compensated for the rudeness of her husband Abel by sending presents to David, describing herself frequently as his 'handmaid'. David took a fancy to her, and when Abel died she became one of his wives.

Abominable Snowman, the: the yeti (Tibetan), an unidentified creature of the Himalayas about which there are many legends. It is said to raid mountain villages and to be tall, powerful and bearlike, with a near-human face. The name was popularised by climbing expeditions in the 1950s and in 1960 Sir Edmund Hillary found footprints which seemed to be those of an animal such as a bear. Legends of mysterious creatures high in the mountains persist and it is suggested that in these days of conservation of dying species the 'snowman' may need protection.

Abraham Men: demented beggars, later imposters; sometimes called 'bedlam beggars'. Bethlehem Hospital (Bedlam), London, the first lunatic asylum in England, established in 1403, had wards named after saints and patriarchs, and inmates in Abraham ward being less violent than the others were allowed to go about the streets begging in the sixteenth and seventeenth centuries. They wore a badge of identification. Others unassociated with the hospital feigned lunacy to attract public sympathy — and money.

Accidental President, the: (1) John Tyler (1790—1862) only became the 10th US President (1841—5) as a result of William Henry Harrison's death, one month after taking office. He did not win a second term. Also known as **His Accidency.** See also *Old Man Eloquent*.

(2) Millard Fillmore. See *the American Louis-Philippe*.

Action Man: Charles, Prince of Wales (b.1948), was noted, prior to marriage, for his enthusiastic sporting activities in many fields. Coupled with his active service in the Royal Navy, such expenditure of energy caused him to be nicknamed after a boy's toy figure which could be dressed in various military gear.

See also *One-Take* and 'PRIVATE EYE' NICKNAMES.

Adolf: see GOSSIP COLUMN NICKNAMES.

Adonis: a dandy, a handsome man (or one who thinks himself so); from the beautiful youth in Greek mythology whom Aphrodite fell in love with. Leigh Hunt dared to call the Prince Regent (later George IV) 'fat Adonis of fifty', but this was only one of several nicknames for the monarch. See *Prinny*.

agony aunt: see *sob sister*.

albert: a short watch-chain fastened to a waistcoat button got this name from Prince Albert, Consort to Queen Victoria, who also gave a similar nickname to a style of frock coat which he favoured.

Alderman, the: see CRICKETERS.

ale-wife: landlady of a tavern or ale-house. The sisterhood produced memorable characters, including a certain Mother Bunce of Cornhill, London, in the late sixteenth century, about whom there were many legends. She was even said to have lived to be 175.

Algy Cluff: see GOSSIP COLUMN NICKNAMES.

Almighty Nose: see *Nosey*.

Alte, der: ('The Old Man') Konrad Adenauer (1876–1967), Chancellor of West Germany who was 73 when he took office in 1949 and served for another fourteen years.

amazons: strong, muscular women, in sport or other activities; sometimes lightly used for female supremacy or success in a job or profession once the prerogative of men. The Amazons in Greek legend were female warriors from Scythia, led by ruthless queens, allowing no men in their ranks and finding fathers for their children from other tribes, rearing only girls. They were said to cut off their right breasts so as to use their bows more efficiently — hence the Greek word for these magnificent women, *amazonides*, breastless.

Ambling Alp, the: see BOXERS.

Ameche: a telephone, from the name of the actor Don Ameche who played the title role in the 1939 film of *The Story of Alexander Graham Bell*, inventor thereof.

American Caesar, the: (1) Ulysses S. Grant. See *the Butcher*.
  (2) Douglas MacArthur (1880–1964), grandiose American general in the Pacific during the Second World War ('I shall return') and then in Korea. Dismissed for insubordination by President Truman.

American Cincinnatus/ Fabius, the: see *the Father of His Country*.

American Dictator, the: see *the Boss*.

American Louis-Philippe, the: Millard Fillmore (1800–74), 13th US President (1850–3), acquired this comparison with the French King (who reigned 1830–48) because of his aristocratic and courteous ways — also because of a supposed physical resemblance. Fillmore was known as **an Accidental President** and **His Accidency** because he only assumed the presidency when Zachary Taylor died in office.

American Sphinx, the: see *the Butcher*.

America's Boy Friend: see FILM STARS.

America's First Gentleman: see *the Dude President*.

America's Sweetheart: see FILM STARS.

Anatomic Bomb, the: see FILM STARS.

Anderson: British air raid shelter in the Second World War, after Sir John Anderson, Home Secretary and Minister of Home Security, 1939—40.

angels: theatrical nickname for those who venture financial backing for stage productions (one of the best methods of losing money ever invented). A suggested origin for the term is that Luis de Santangel was the man who actually put up the money for Christopher Columbus's voyage to America. However, a derivation from 'guardian angel' would seem adequate.

angry young men: writers of the 1950s who showed a social awareness and expressed dissatisfaction with conventional values and with the 'Establishment'. The term derived in part from use in connection with *Look Back in Anger*, a play by John Osborne in 1956, but Leslie Paul, a social philosopher, had called his autobiography *Angry Young Man* in 1951. Applied in later years to youthful literary 'protesters' generally.

Animated Meringue, the: Barbara Cartland (b.1901), romantic novelist and health food champion, has employed a chalky style of make-up in addition to driving around in a *pink* and white Rolls-Royce. She was thus dubbed by Arthur Marshall who says that, far from taking offence, Miss Cartland sent him a telegram of thanks. Sometimes labelled **the World's Most Prolific Novelist**.

Anthony Eden: a black felt hat popularised in the 1930s by Sir Anthony Eden (later Lord Avon) when he was Foreign Secretary and one of the best-dressed members of the House of Commons.

Anzacs: members of the Australian and New Zealand Army Corps who fought in the First World War and especially at Gallipoli. The name is formed from the initials. Anzac Day in both countries is 25 April, commemorating the landing on the beaches exposed to Turkish fire in 1915.

Ape: see *the Emancipator*.

Attila of Sunnybrook Farm: see FILM STARS.

Attila the Hen: see *the Iron Lady*.

Aunt Edna: during the revolution in English drama of the 1950s, this term was called into play by the new wave of angry young dramatists and their supporters to describe the more conservative kind of theatre-goer − the type who preferred comfortable three-act plays of the Shaftesbury Avenue kind. Ironically, the term had been coined in self-defence by Terence Rattigan, one of the previous generation of dramatists.

In the preface to Volume II of his *Collected Plays* (1953) he wrote of: 'A nice respectable, middle-class, middle-aged maiden lady, with time on her hands and the money to help her pass it . . . Let us call her Aunt Edna . . . Now Aunt Edna does not appreciate Kafka . . . She is, in short, a hopeless lowbrow . . . Aunt Edna is universal, and to those who feel that all the problems of the modern theatre might be saved by her liquidation, let me add that . . . She is also immortal.'

Auntie: the British Broadcasting Corporation, so dubbed mockingly by newspaper columnists, television critics and employees, becoming familiar from 1954 at the start of commercial television, the BBC supposedly staid and unambitious by comparison. A BBC spokesman countered with, 'An auntie is often a much-loved member of the family.' The Corporation assimilated the nickname to such effect that when arrangements were made to supply wine to BBC clubs in London direct from vineyards in Burgundy it was bottled under the label *Tantine*.

In 1979, the comedian Arthur Askey suggested to one of the authors that he had originated the term during the *Band Waggon* programme in the late 1930s. While quite probably he did, the widespread use of the nickname is more likely to have arisen as suggested above.

Also **the Beeb**, notably after the inception of Radio 1, the pop music network, in 1967 and perhaps coined by Kenny Everett.

Awfully Weirdly: play upon the name of Aubrey Beardsley (1872—98), the stylised English illustrator. Also **Daubaway Weirdsley**.

Ayrshire Poet, the: Robert Burns (1759—96), born at Alloway, Ayrshire.

B

Babe, the: (or **the Bambino**) 'Babe' (George Herman) Ruth (1895−1948), US professional baseball-player. The basic nickname arose when he joined his first team at the comparatively early age of 19. He became known as **the Sultan of Swat** in about 1920 because of the way he slugged at the ball. There had been a real Sultan (or, more properly, Akhoond) of Swat, now part of Pakistan, in the 1870s whose death gave rise to doggerel by George Lanigans and Edward Lear.

Babes in the Wood, the: Irish ruffians who ranged the Wicklow mountains and the Enniscorthy woods towards the end of the eighteenth century − one of the many mellifluous nicknames adopted by Irish gangs or protest groups: these included **Molly Maguires** who wore women's clothes to surprise and combat rent collectors and fight eviction; **Oak Boys**, active against tithes, wearing oak leaves in their hats; **Peep o'day Boys**, a Protestant secret society which carried out dawn raids against Catholic homes; **Steelboys** who rampaged in Ulster to protest against tithes; and **Whiteboys** with similar grievances as well as opposition to the enclosure system, wearing white frocks over their clothes as disguise and group identification.

Bachelor President, the: see *Old Public Functionary.*

backroom boys: scientists and boffins generally, as identified by the Services in the Second World War and relied on to produce inventions and new gadgets for weaponry and navigation. Lord Beaverbrook originated the term *in this sense* when he was Minister of Supply in 1941 and referred in a broadcast to the 'boys in the backroom'. He was inspired to do so by Marlene Dietrich's singing of 'The Boys in the Backroom' from the film *Destry Rides Again.*

Badger: see 'PRIVATE EYE' NICKNAMES.

Baillie, the/Baillie Vass: see 'PRIVATE EYE' NICKNAMES.

Baker, the: (1) Louis XVI (1754–93), because of the bread that he and Marie Antoinette doled out to the mob at Versailles, 1789, and translated thus in English newspapers; hence the Queen's nickname of **the Baker's Wife**. (2) Jack Martin. See under BOXERS.

Bald Eagle of Foggy Bottom, the: any American, bald and austere, is likely to attract comparison with the bald eagle, national symbol of the United States. This particular name was applied to Robert Lovett (b.1895), President Truman's Secretary of Defense, who was notably bald. He had earlier worked in the State Department which was nicknamed Foggy Bottom for its habit of obfuscation (though this was the original name of the land on which it is situated in Washington DC).

Congressman Tristram Burges (1770–1853), had earlier been known as **the Bald Eagle of Rhode Island** (which he represented).

Baldilocks: see 'PRIVATE EYE' NICKNAMES.

Bambino, the: see *the Babe*.

Banana King, the: Roger Ackerley (1863–1929), chief salesman of Elders & Fyffes, banana importers. He helped Britain become 'banana-conscious' in the early years of the twentieth century.

Banbury-man: a zealous Puritan, preaching and admonishing, of whom there were said to be many in this Oxfordshire town in the seventeenth century. They were satirised by contemporary writers, including Ben Jonson in *Bartholomew Fair*.

Banjo or **the Banjo:** Andrew Barton Paterson (1864–1941), Australian journalist and poet. He wrote the words for 'Waltzing Matilda'.

Bank of America's Sweetheart, the: see FILM STARS.

Bard (of Avon), the: William Shakespeare (1564−1616) − one of several names of tribute alluding to the river running through his birthplace at Stratford in Warwickshire. Ben Jonson called him **Sweet Swan of Avon** (in a verse prefacing the First Folio of Shakespeare's plays, 1623) and David Garrick, who excelled in Shakespearean parts at Drury Lane Theatre, London, felt intimate enough to nickname him **Avonian Willy**. 'The Bard' on its own is also, unfortunately, common though anything is better than the assumed familiarity of 'Will' Shakespeare.

barker: front-man at a fairground show, attracting attention by loud and descriptive language, or anyone luring custom in similar fashion; the analogy is presumably with a noisy dog. The nickname has been given in the USA to a baseball coach.

barnstormer: a flamboyant or second-rate actor, originating from the 'strolling players' who toured country districts and performed on village greens or in barns, suiting their style to the audience and location.

Baron Bonkers: see GOSSIP COLUMN NICKNAMES.

Basher Bainbridge: Beryl Bainbridge (b.1934), the novelist, was so named at school near Liverpool *c*.1946 because of her propensity for bashing up people (boys and girls). She commented to us (1984): 'I was a terrible fighter at school and the culmination was when I challenged twenty-five girls to a fight by the lily pond. I pushed one of them in. It was a game; they weren't my enemies. The name stuck to me all through my schooldays. I've never told it to anyone since.'

Her brother, Ian, also suffered alliteratively. He was called 'Batty' Bainbridge.

Bathing Towel: 1st Baron Baden-Powell (1857−1941), founder of the Boy Scout movement, acquired this obvious rhyming nickname during his schooldays at Charterhouse.

Batman: see *Mr Clean*.

Beard, the: see FILM STARS.

Beast, the: see 'PRIVATE EYE' NICKNAMES.

Beast of Belsen, the: Josef Kramer (1906–45), commandant of Belsen concentration camp during the worst period of its history from December 1944 to the end of the war. He was executed for his crimes.

Beast of Bolsover, the: Dennis Skinner (b.1932), aggressive and outspoken Left-wing Labour MP for Bolsover in Derbyshire from 1970, acquired this nickname from parliamentary correspondents (possibly at the time of *the Beast of Jersey*). He is a former miner. Noted for interrupting speeches and making loud comments, he has several times been asked by the Speaker of the House of Commons to leave the Chamber because of his behaviour.

Beast of Jersey, the: E. J. L. (Ted) Paisnel was convicted of thirteen sex offences against children and sentenced to thirty years' imprisonment in 1971. The name was applied to him during the eleven years he evaded arrest on the island.

Beast 666, the: (or **the Great Beast**) Aleister Crowley (*c*.1876–1947), satanist, who experimented in necromancy and the black arts, sex and drugs. He called himself the mystical 'Beast 666' after the man referred to in *Revelation*, 13:18: 'Let him that hath understanding count the number of the beast: for it is the number of a man: and his number is six hundred threescore and six.' Newspapers called Crowley the **Wickedest Man in the World** though he fell short of proving the claim.

beatniks: young people who opted out of normal society in the 1950s, unable or unwilling to conform to conventional standards or with the stress of ordinary life. They congregated in groups, careless of appearance, usually down-at-heel, critical of the 'Establishment', often getting into trouble with the law. The name indicated a 'beat' generation, with a Yiddish or Russian suffix (cf. the Russian *sputnik*, satellite orbiting the earth in 1957). They were less intellectual than the *angry young men*, but rebellious like *Teddy Boys* who preceded them, and hippies who followed, each with different connotations.

Beau Brummell: George Bryan Brummell (1778–1840), dandy and leader of fashion in London society. His taste in clothes was evidenced at Eton and Oxford, and when he inherited a fortune he set himself up as an arbiter of male fashion, encouraged by his friends who also valued his witty conversation, his aplomb and conceit. The Prince of Wales was one of his friendly admirers — for a time. He is credited with the rude remark about the future George IV, 'Who is your fat friend?' He lost his money by gambling and extravagance, and both his health and appearance deteriorated sadly. His nickname has also been applied to any dandy or fop, but Brummell had an excellent sartorial taste.

Beau Nash: Richard Nash (1674–1762), famed as master of ceremonies at Bath which, under his strict and imaginative jurisdiction, enhanced its reputation as a fashionable spa. He introduced rules for balls and assemblies, forbade the wearing of swords and boots in public places, brought duelling into disrepute, cleaned up the streets and introduced a tariff for lodgings. His dress and trappings suited his status, wearing a large white hat and richly embroidered coat, and driving about town in a carriage with six horses and uniformed grooms blowing French horns. Also: **the King of Bath**.

Beaver, the: (1) William Maxwell Aitken, 1st Baron Beaverbrook (1879–1964), newspaper magnate and politician, who took his title from the town in New Brunswick, Canada, where he had a home. Called 'Max' by his friends, he was known to his staff as 'the beaver', explained by Tom Driberg (his first William Hickey columnist on the *Daily Express*) as 'a zoological symbol of tireless industry'. To some critics he was known as **Robin Badfellow** — more in amusement than in anger.

(2) Simone de Beauvoir (b.1908), the French novelist, was called 'Beaver' by her lover, Jean-Paul Sartre, the existen-

tialist philosopher. Clearly an English language play upon her surname. By others she was known as **Notre Dame de Sartre**.

Beeb, the: see *Auntie*.

beefeaters: Yeomen of the Guard who have attended English state occasions since the coronation of Henry VII in 1485. Their duties included being at royal banquets at which they probably tucked into the 'left-overs'. They would have had access to the kitchens and been given a generous food allowance, hence the nickname for well-fed state servants. The nickname probably arose to distinguish them from 'loaf-eaters', as more menial servants were known. Warders at the Tower of London have also been known as beefeaters since the seventeenth century. (Cf. *doughboy* on the coincidence of that name with soldiers' payment in food.)

Bela Lugosi of American Politics, the: see *Tricky Dick*.

belcher: a blue scarf with white spots, current from the early nineteenth century because such neckwear was sported by James 'Jem' Belcher (1781–1811), a pugilistic favourite during his short career. His last fight in 1809 was with Tom Cribb who defeated him. He had been a butcher, but he retired from the ring to become a publican.

Belfast Spider, the: see BOXERS.

Belisha beacon: a yellow glass globe atop a pole marked in black and white bands and situated on both sides of a pedestrian crossing as a warning to motorists; introduced when Leslie Hore-Belisha (created a Baron, 1954) was Minister of Transport, 1934–7.

Bell-the-Cat: Archibald Douglas, 5th Earl of Angus (*c*.1450–1514) who earned the nickname by devising a scheme to get rid of Robert Cochrane, hated favourite of James III of Scotland. He is reputed to have said that he would 'bell the cat', and he began the attack by pulling Cochrane's gold chain from his neck. Cochrane and others were hanged.

Douglas switched his allegiance, and was a leader in the rebellion against James.

Bendigo: see BOXERS.

Bendor: 2nd Duke of Westminster (1879–1953). The nickname commemorates a defeat in heraldic law for his ancestor, Sir Robert Grosvenor, over the coat of arms he could bear. In 1389 the Court of Chivalry ruled in favour of Sir Richard le Scrope in his action over the right to arms 'Azure, a bend or' (a blue shield with a diagonal gold bar). Grosvenor refused to accept this and appealed to Richard II. The monarch also ruled against him and Grosvenor was forced to bear the costs of the action. He ended up using 'Azure, a garb or' (a blue shield with a golden sheaf of corn).

Benicia Boy, the: see BOXERS.

Bennery: see *Wedgie.*

Bennies: inhabitants of the Falkland Islands, so named by British forces stationed there, following the 1982 conflict with Argentina. The uncomplimentary reference was to a not-very-bright character called 'Bennie' in the TV soap opera *Crossroads.* When reprimanded, troops resorted instead to calling the islanders **Stills** (i.e. 'Still Bennies'.) A still later variant by sections of the occupying forces, for some of the islanders, was **Bubs** — for 'Bloody Ungrateful Bastards'. The islanders responded by calling the soldiers **Whennies** after their constant references to past exploits: 'When I was in Belize, when I was in Cyprus . . .'

Bertie: see *Tum-Tum.*

Beryl: see POP STARS.

Bess of Hardwick: see *Building Bess.*

Bevin boys: young men in the United Kingdom who were directed to work in the coal mines during the Second World War instead of being conscripted into the Services. The measure was introduced in 1942 by Ernest Bevin who was Minister of Labour and National Service. See *the dockers' KC*.

Big Ben: the bell in the clock tower of the Houses of Parliament, London, weighing 13½ tons, named after Sir Benjamin Hall, Commissioner of Works when it was hung in 1856.

Big Bertha: soldiers' nickname for the German long-range gun in the First World War, used to shell Paris in 1918. Bertha, only child of Friedrich Alfred Krupp (1854–1902) who had inherited the great engineering and armaments undertaking, married in 1906 and her husband became head of the firm.

Big Bill: William Hale Thompson (1867–1944), urban demagogue and three times Mayor of Chicago. Running for his third term in 1927, Thompson whipped up anglophobia and threatened that if King George V ever set foot in the city he would 'bust (or punch) him on the snoot'. The King wisely kept away and protected his proboscis.

Big Cyril: Cyril Smith (b.1928), Liberal MP for Rochdale from 1972. A large, sometimes genial and forceful personality, weighing 25 stone, at one time.

Big Daddy: (1) Lyndon B. Johnson (1908–73), 36th President of the USA (1963–9) – known much more widely, however, by his initials, LBJ.
(2) Idi Amin (b.1925), massively built President of Uganda and dictator (1971–9), known to his people as 'Idi Amin Dada'.
(3) The stage name of Shirley Crabtree (b.1936), British all-in wrestler (male).

Big Enchilada, the: John Mitchell (b.1913), US Attorney-General who led President Nixon's re-election campaign in 1972 and subsequently was sentenced to a gaol term for associated offences. An enchilada is a Mexican dish. The term was evoked (like 'Big Cheese') by a Nixon aide, John Erlichman, during a 1973 taped conversation in the White

House. He sought to describe the size of the sacrificial victim who was being thrown to the wolves.

Biggles: see 'PRIVATE EYE' NICKNAMES.

Big-Hearted Arthur: Arthur Askey, British comedian (1900–82). 'I have always used this expression about myself,' said Askey in 1979, 'even when I was at school. When playing cricket, if the ball was hit to the boundary and nobody would go and fetch it, I would, saying, "Big-hearted Arthur, that's me!"' The phrase was used in the first edition of radio's *Band Waggon* in 1938 and the self-applied tag stayed with him as billing for the rest of his life.

Big Jim: see GANGSTERS.

Biglips: see 'PRIVATE EYE' NICKNAMES.

Big Mal: Malcolm Fraser (b.1930), Australian Prime Minister (1975–83). This was one of the kinder epithets attracted by Fraser, over 6 feet tall and abrasive in manner.

Big Three, the: Churchill, Roosevelt and Stalin, heads of government of the UK, US and USSR in the Second World War, so called when they met in conference at Yalta, 1945. It had also been applied to Woodrow Wilson, David Lloyd George and Georges Clemenceau at the 1919 Versailles Peace Conference.

Big Yin, the: see SHOW BUSINESS STARS.

Billy Blue: Sir William Cornwallis (1744–1819), British admiral who was popular enough among his sailors to earn several nicknames beside this one – **Billy-Go-Tight** (probably because of his ruddy complexion), **Coachee** and **Mr Whip**. He fought the French fleet in the West Indies and in the Channel, usually against heavy odds, and he became a temporary hero in 1795 when in action off Brest he was surrounded but managed to escape, and yet he turned back to rescue one of his badly damaged frigates.

billycock: this nickname for a hat (the American 'derby') links us with a person — William Coke of Norfolk, from whom we also get 'coke' for the same headgear, and these in turn introduce a Huguenot family which provided another nickname. See *bowler* for explanation.

Billy-Go-Tight: see *Billy Blue*.

Bing/ Der Bingle: see *the Old Groaner*.

Binkie: Hugh Beaumont (1908—73), managing director of H. M. Tennant, the theatre group. He was the most influential force in West End theatre from the 1940s to the 1970s. He was always known thus within the profession. He disliked the name Hugh. Perhaps the nickname came from his childhood. One cannot help hearing an echo of 'Dandie Dinmont' (the terrier named after a character in one of Sir Walter Scott's novels).

Biograph Girl, the: see FILM STARS.

Bird: see JAZZ MUSICIANS.

Bitch of Buchenwald, the: Ilse Koch (d.1967), wife of the Commandant of Buchenwald, the Nazi concentration camp during the Second World War.

Black and Tans, the: members of a special armed force (made up of ex-servicemen) sent to Ireland in 1920 by the British Government. Their purpose was to put down Republican rebels which they attempted to do with much bloodshed. Derived from the colour of their mixed uniforms — army khaki combined with the black belts and dark green caps of the Royal Irish Constabulary — but also from the name of a pack of hounds in County Limerick. Earlier, during the Reconstruction period after the American Civil War, the name had been given to Republicans unwilling to abandon the negro as a basis of the party's power in Alabama.

Black Boy, the: see *the Merry Monarch*.

Black Diamond, the: see BOXERS.

Black Douglas: James, Lord of Douglas (1286–1330), so called by the English for his raids on the border, and perhaps because of the way he captured Roxburgh castle in 1314 by disguising his men as black oxen. Two years later he slew Sir Robert de Nevill, 'Peacock of the North', in single combat. He fought on the side of Robert Bruce and is romanticised in Scottish history for his dash and daring. He died fighting the Moors in Spain.

There is an interesting 'black' connection with the noble family of Douglas, the name originating from the Gaelic *dubh glas*, dark water.

Black Jack: (1) John Philip Kemble (1757–1823), the handsome dark-haired actor who was noted for his tragic Shakespearean parts, including that of Hamlet. He was brother of Sarah Siddons, **the Tragedy Queen of the British Stage.**

(2) US General John Joseph Pershing (1860–1948), commander-in-chief of the American Expeditionary Force in the First World War. Earlier in his career he had led black troops in Cuba and the Philippines.

black maria: police van, painted black. There has been much speculation about 'maria'. It may be connected with the notorious murder of a girl called Maria Marten, for which a man was hanged in 1828. Maria and the red barn in which her body was found became subjects of plays and stories, and the most notable melodrama, produced in London in 1840, is part of theatrical history. An American explanation for the name is that a brawny negress called Maria Lee who kept a lodging house in Boston helped the police to bundle arrested people into the van. The term was current in the USA by 1847.

Black Panther, the: Donald Neilsen, convicted of the kidnap and murder of Lesley Whittle and of the killing of three subpost office officials in 1975. He was so dubbed by the popular press during the nine-month police search for him on account of the black hood he wore to disguise himself. The inadvisability of the indiscriminate use of such sobriquets was demonstrated during Neilsen's trial when a BBC Radio 4 newsreader announced: 'At Oxford, a jury has been told that Donald Nielsen denied he was the *Pink* Panther.'

Black Prince, the: Edward, Prince of Wales (1330–76), eldest son of Edward III. He fought with distinction at the battles of Crécy and Poitiers and gained his nickname because of his black armour.

Blackshirts: uniformed fascist followers of Benito Mussolini in Italy and of Adolf Hitler in Germany, but usually applied to the former who became active in the 1920s. Hitler's blackshirts (the SS) came into prominence in the 1930s. The black shirt became a symbol of fascism, and in England it was worn by followers of Sir Oswald Mosley who re-formed his New Party into the British Union of Fascists.

Blanketeers: Lancashire handloom weavers, spinners and other cotton and wool operatives, impoverished by changing industrial conditions, who assembled on St Peter's field, Manchester (later scene of the 'Peterloo Massacre') in 1817 to march to London to petition the Prince Regent. Each carried a blanket for the planned several days' journey. They did not get far, however, before they were dispersed, and their leaders imprisoned. They set the pattern for more spectacular demonstrations over the years and nicknamed 'hunger marches', including the 'Jarrow Crusade' in 1936 (a march of unemployed shipyard workers from County Durham to London) and a similar one from Glasgow in 1983.

Blessed Arnold Goodman, the: see 'PRIVATE EYE' NICKNAMES.

Blessed Margaret, the: see *the Iron Lady*.

Blind Poet, the: John Milton (1608–74) was appointed Latin Secretary to the Council of State in 1649 and five years later became blind. His greatest poems, *Paradise Lost* and *Paradise Regained* were composed during his blindness. As an undergraduate at Cambridge, according to John Aubrey, 'He was so faire that they called him **the Lady of Christ's College**'.

Bloody Mary: Mary I (1516–58), daughter of Henry VIII and Catherine of Aragon, who re-established Roman Catholicism in England when she succeeded her brother, Edward VI. There was persecution of Protestants, and about 300 opponents of 'the old faith' were executed, hence the popular nickname.

bloomers: a female fashion of a skirt reaching to just below the knees and under which were wide trousers, gathered at the ankles. A close-fitting jacket usually completed the ensemble. The fashion was introduced in New York – though not invented – by Mrs Amelia Jenks Bloomer around 1851, and it was soon adopted in England where it had a sensational vogue for a time and delighted cartoonists. The trousers were especially appropriate for younger ladies taking up the recreation of bicycling, and the word became a nickname for these nether garments, then as they disappeared under longer skirts it was applied to the underwear which for long preceded knickers and panties.

Bloomsbury Group (Circle or Set), the: a coterie of literary and artistic people who lived in and around that district of London before and after the First World War, meeting to discuss their own and others' work, propound ideas, eminently self-aware and adulatory, often defying convention. They included Leonard and Virginia Woolf, Maynard Keynes, Lytton Strachey, Roger Fry, E. M. Forster, Duncan Grant, Vanessa and Clive Bell. The group has been a profitable source of innumerable biographies and reminiscences, so that more than one reviewer has exclaimed, 'What – not another!'

Bluejackets: British sailors, from the nineteenth century. Colour of uniforms has produced many nicknames: cf. *redcoats* and the various 'shirts'. Federal soldiers of the American Civil War were called **Bluebellies** by the Confederates because of their light blue overcoats and cloaks, and in return the latter were named **Greybacks**, alluding to their grey uniforms. An RAF nickname for a khaki-clad soldier was **Brown-job**.

Blue-Ribbonites, the: (or **the Blue Ribbon Army**) nineteenth-century crusaders against intoxicating liquor in the USA, identified by a slip of blue ribbon on their coat lapels, blouses or arms. The movement spread to Britain where in 1883 it took the name of the Gospel Temperance Union.

Blueshirts: Irishmen who volunteered to fight for General Franco in the Spanish Civil War, 1936–9.

Bluestockings: literary or studious women, from the gatherings of cultivated females and a few eminent men who met in various places but especially at the home of Elizabeth Montagu in Mayfair, London, a leader of society who encouraged discussion of the latest books and poems instead of banter and gossip over games of cards. These intellectual conversaziones began around 1750 and the playful nicknames of 'Bluestocking ladies' and 'bluestocking clubs' are explained by Boswell in his *Life of Johnson.* He says that a certain Benjamin Stillingfleet, expert on natural history, was a popular guest, soberly dressed but wearing blue stockings. 'Such was the excellence of his conversation, that his absence was felt as so great a loss, that it used to be said, "We can do nothing without the blue stockings", and thus by degrees the title was established.' Dr Johnson, who was very fond of the ladies, attended the sessions himself. It is also said that Mrs Montagu and her coterie took to wearing blue stockings.

Boanerges: nickname given by Jesus (and one of several indications of his humour) to James and John, sons of Zebedee, who were over-enthusiastic in their condemnation of opponents. The Greek translation from a Hebrew word means 'sons of thunder' or of 'riot', thus mocking their loud invective (*Mark*, 3:17; *Luke*, 9:54). The word was adopted in English for a noisily intense preacher or public speaker.

Boar, the: Richard III (1452–85), because of the boar on his heraldic cognizance — 'the wretched, bloody and usurping boar', as Shakespeare called it in the play about the king (V:ii). Another of his nicknames was **Crookback**, perhaps

because of a deformed spine, although contemporary portraits do not show it, and he was described as 'comely'. He
probably walked with a stoop, and this has since been
exaggerated by dramatists, from Shakespeare onward.
Shakespeare makes him say:

> Then, since the heavens have shaped my body so,
> Let hell make crook'd my mind to answer it.

Great efforts have been made in recent years to contradict
calumny about him, and a Richard III Society extolls his
virtues and defends his reputation.

bobby: British policeman, from Sir Robert Peel who, as
Home Secretary, established the Metropolitan Police Force
in 1829. The nickname gradually superseded *peeler*, adopted
earlier in his career when he was Secretary for Ireland and
founded the Irish constabulary, although 'peeler' lingered
long in the underworld.

bobby-soxers: American schoolgirls and teenagers generally
who wore short white socks in the 1940s. Such socks were
identified with exuberant youth for several years, and the
British press used the name for noisy teenagers at dances
and early post-war 'pop' concerts.

Bobs: Frederick Sleigh Roberts, 1st Earl Roberts (1832–1914),
noted Field Marshal. He spent over forty years in India,
including distinguished service in the Mutiny (for which he
was awarded the VC) and his famous march from Kabul to
Kandahar. In 1900 he commanded the British forces in South
Africa and brought the controversial war to an end. Queen
Victoria received him at her last audience before her death.

Not just a simple diminutive, though 'Bob' is short for
'Robert' and thus Bobs/Roberts – 'Bobs Bahadur' is Hindu-
stani for 'hero' or 'champion'.

The Irish Guards came to be known as 'Bob's Own', as he
had been the first Colonel of the regiment.

Body, the: see FILM STARS.

boffins: scientists and inventors, probably of RAF origin in the Second World War but adopted in other Services. Such men produced navigational aids and bomb-aiming and gunnery gadgetry. There was an eccentric gentleman called Mr Boffin in Dickens's *Our Mutual Friend*.

Bogey: see FILM STARS.

Bombardier Billy Wells: see BOXERS.

Bomber Harris: Marshal of the Royal Air Force Sir Arthur Harris Bt (1892—1984), aggressive commander-in-chief of Bomber Command in the Second World War and advocate of strategic bombing. He directed the great bomber offensive from Britain, a relentless night-by-night attack on German cities and manufacturing centres, ports and railways, and on other enemy territory. His policy has since been criticised and its effects questioned. Known as 'Butch' or 'Bert' to his colleagues, the 'Bomber' bit came from a more public perception.

Bones: see *the Gov'nor*.

Boney: Napoleon I (Napoleon Bonaparte) (1769—1821), Emperor of the French (1804—15). The nickname was used in derision or to keep courage up from 1798 when he seemed to be threatening an invasion of Britain. In his own country he was affectionately nicknamed **the Little Corporal** ('le Petit Caporal') recalling his humble (but very short) period in an artillery regiment: he quickly became an officer. He was not as 'little' as all that — 5 feet 6 inches tall. Describing his appearance in his last years on St Helena, Major-General Frank Richardson in *Napoleon's Death: an Inquest* (William Kimber, 1974) says: ' . . . his corpulence and fat round thighs made him look shorter than he really was. His legs were quite shapely and he was proud of his delicate little hands and feet.'

Later he became known as **the Violet Corporal** when he was defeated by the allied armies in 1814 and allowed to live in exile on the Mediterranean island of Elba. He told his followers that he would return to France with the violets, which he did, although a little early, escaping from Elba in February 1815. He was also dubbed **the Man of Destiny** and Bernard Shaw used this as title for a play about him.

Bonnie Prince Charlie: see *the Young Pretender*.

Boofy: 8th Earl of Arran (1910−83), politician and journalist.

Bosie: (1) Lord Alfred Douglas (1870−1945), poet and Oscar Wilde's friend − indeed, the ultimate cause of the writer's downfall. He was known to all his friends as 'Bosie' − a corruption of 'Boysie', the name given to him as a child by his indulgent mother.

(2) Australian cricketing nickname from the 1900s for the googly, a method of bowling a cricket ball, named after its inventor, the Middlesex and England player, Bernard Bosanquet.

Boss, the: (1) Franklin D. Roosevelt (1882−1945), 32nd President of the USA (1933−45). During nearly four full terms in office, he acquired a whole catalogue of nicknames, although principally referred to by his initials, FDR. **Sphinx** was used because he could be inscrutable; **the Squire of Hyde Park** reflected that he lived like a country squire on his estate at Hyde Park, NY; **That (Mad) Man in the White House** was employed by opponents too displeased even to mention his name. He was hailed by Democrats as **the Gallant Leader** and **the Gideon of Democracy**. Republicans called him **the New Deal Caesar, the Raw Dealocrat, the American Dictator, the Feather-Duster of Dutchess County, Kanga-roosevelt,** and **Franklin Deficit Roosevelt. Houdini in the White House** reflected his ability to get out of difficult situations.

(2) Bess Truman (1885−1982), wife of President Harry S. Truman.

(3) Margaret Thatcher. See *the Iron Lady*.

Boston Strangler, the: Albert de Salvo, who strangled thirteen women during 1962−4 in the Boston, Mass. area.

Boston Strong Boy, the: see BOXERS.

Boswell, a: a biographer, especially an adulatory one, as was James Boswell, adoring biographer of Dr Johnson. See *Bozzy*.

Bottomless Pitt, the: the inevitable nickname for anyone named Pitt. It was certainly applied to William Pitt the Younger (1759—1806), British Prime Minister (1783—1801, 1804—6). A caricature attributed to Gillray with this title shows Pitt as Chancellor of the Exchequer introducing his 1792 budget. His bottom is non-existent.

Bouncing Czech, the: see GOSSIP COLUMN NICKNAMES.

bowler: eponymous nickname for a low-crowned hard hat, introduced by William Coke of Norfolk in 1850 to replace his high riding hat as more suitable for hunting; a kind of smart crash-helmet designed by a well-known hatter, Mr Beaulieu, one of a family of such craftsmen in Stockport and London who anglicised their Huguenot name to Bowler. As the fashion spread the nicknames commemorated the inventor, e.g. 'coke' and 'billycock'. But 'bowler' has become the longest lasting, and its American equivalent of 'derby', so called because pictures of Lord Derby at races and other outdoor functions showed him wearing such a hat.

bowler-hatted bull: British farmers' nickname for a Ministry of Agriculture representative or veterinary surgeon who artificially inseminates cows.

BOXERS: It has long been the custom for boxers to be kitted out with an alternative or additional name which (a) promotes them to the public (like entertainers) and (b) begins to cow their opponents even before they step into the ring together. The fashion began with the bare-knuckle fighters at the end of the eighteenth and beginning of the nineteenth century. One of the first to earn a nickname was John Jackson — **Gentleman Jack** or **Jackson** — English champion from 1795 to 1803 and who, on his retirement, took up a successful career as instructor and taught Byron to box. Hence his lines:

> And men unpractised in exchanging knocks
> Must go to Jackson ere they dare to box.

Some of these pugilists (aptly named 'bruisers' and 'prize-fighters') were named after their trade, as was Tom Hickman, **the Gasman**, or **Gas-lightman**, from Worcestershire, boastful winner of many a fight and darling of 'the fancy' until he was defeated in 1821 by Bill Neat. Hazlitt devoted an essay to this gory contest, and a verse of the time read:

> In eighteen rounds the Gas was spent,
> His pipes lay undefended,
> When Gas-light shares fell cent by cent,
> And thus the battle ended.

Another was Jack Martin, **the Baker**, or **Master of the Rolls**. Other nicknames have just been variants on the 'Kid' theme or merely indicated the boxer's place of birth — **Jersey Joe** Walcott, for example, or **the Prime Irish Lad** (Jack Randall, also known as **the Nonpareil**, who won the lightweight title over twenty-nine rounds in 1817.)

Everyone knew who **the Black Diamond** was — Tom Cribb, the Gloucestershire coal-porter, who was beaten only once in a long career. He twice beat James Belcher (known always and affectionately as 'Jem' and as **the Bristol Butcher**, which was his trade until he retired to become a publican), and was champion in his class from 1809 to 1848. Henry ('Hen') Pearce, known as **the Game Chicken**, was a pupil of Belcher whom he defeated in an epic fight in 1805.

The fashion for boxing nicknames has been kept up into modern times. Here is a selection of the more distinctive labels:

Belfast Spider, the: Ike Weir, a Scotsman, was the first boxer to be considered world featherweight champion, in the 1880s.
Bendigo: William Thompson, three times English champion between 1839 and 1851.
Benicia Boy, the: John C. Heenan, boxer from Benicia, California, who in 1860 fought for more than two hours with Tom Sayers, the English champion. The contest ended in a draw.
Bombardier Billy Wells: William Wells, heavyweight

champion of England from 1911 until he lost the title to Joe Beckett in 1919. Also provided anyone called Wells with an inseparable nickname.

Boston Strong Boy, the: John L. Sullivan, massive long-distance fighter who lost his American heavyweight championship to Jim Corbett in New Orleans, 1892. American 'Champion of the Universe' in the 1880s.

Brockton Blockbuster, the: another name for Rocky Marciano (born Rocco Marchegiano) (1923–69) from Brockton, Mass., world heavyweight champion 1952–6.

Brown Bomber, the: Joe Louis, world heavyweight champ from 1937 until his retirement in 1949. When he returned to the ring in 1950, he was defeated by Ezzard Charles. He was noted for his large number of knockouts. (The nickname lives on: it was seen applied to a Burmese cat at stud in West London, 1983.)

Fargo Express, the: Billy Petrolle, a lightweight from Fargo, North Dakota, in the 1920s.

Fighting Marine, the: Gene Tunney (who had been with the US Marine Corps in the First World War).

Gentle Giant, the: Larry Holmes (b.1950), world heavyweight champion.

Gentleman Jim: James J. Corbett, American heavyweight champion under the Queensberry Rules, 1892–7.

Hurricane Henry Armstrong: (real name Henry Jackson), American featherweight, lightweight and welterweight champion (simultaneously) in the 1930s. He had a non-stop punching style.

Italian Alp, the: Primo Carnera (1906–67), heavyweight of the 1930s, stood 6 feet 5¾ inches and weighed almost 19 stone. World heavyweight champion from June 1933, when he knocked out Jack Sharkey after six rounds, until June 1934, when he was defeated by Max Baer in eleven rounds, both fights in New York. Also known as **the Ambling Alp.**

Jewel of the Ghetto, the: Ruby Goldstein, American boxer of the early 1900s – later referee – whose nickname not only reflected his first name but also his origins in Manhattan's Lower East Side.

Li'l Arthur: John Arthur Johnson, 6 feet 1 inch first black heavyweight champion, in the 1900s.

Livermore Larruper, the: Max Baer, American heavyweight champion in 1934. To 'larrup' means to beat or thresh. He came from Livermore, California.

Louisville Lip: Muhammad Ali (formerly Cassius Clay) (b.1942) was world heavyweight champion from 1964 when, at the age of 22, he defeated Sonny Liston. His ability to out-talk absolutely anyone earned him this nickname — also **the Mouth**.

Manassa Mauler, the: Jack Dempsey (1895—1983), world heavyweight champion (1919—26), was born in Manassa, Colorado. He first fought as 'Kid' Blackie.

Michigan Assassin, the: Stanley Ketchel, middleweight champion of the 1900s. He had a tendency to make a mess of his opponents.

Orchid Man: Georges Charpentier (1894—1975), French light-heavyweight champion of Europe, debonair and sprightly in the ring. He gained the championship in 1919 by knocking out Joe Beckett in the first round. His attempt to gain the world title failed when he was defeated by Jack Dempsey in 1921. Also known as **Gentleman George**.

Pot(t)awatomie Giant, the: Jess Willard, from Pot(t)awatomie County, Kansas, was the tallest heavyweight most people had seen, in 1915.

Scotch Wop, the: John Dundee, featherweight of the 1920s. His real name was Joseph Carrora.

Slapsie Maxie: Max Rosenbloom, light-heavyweight champ from 1932 to 1934, was known for his slap-like punches.

Smokin' Joe: (or **Smokey Joe**) Joe Frazier (b.1944), black heavyweight champ in 1970, who came out 'smokin' — throwing blows.

Sugar Ray Robinson: (b.1920), five times world middleweight champ in the period of 1940—65. Born Walker Smith, this boxer first used the name of an older friend, Ray Robinson, in order to enter the ring. A journalist commented that the young boxer was 'sweet as sugar', and the name stuck.

Two-Ton: Tony Galento, American heavyweight of the 1930s, was 'built like a beer-keg'.

Wild Bull of the Pampas, the: Luis Angel Firpo, an Argentinian boxer of the 1920s.

Yankee Nigger, the: Tom Molineaux, an American ex-slave who fought in England during the 1810s.

Yankee Sullivan: James Ambrose, a British-born boxer, in the USA during the 1840s.

Boy Browning: Lieut-Gen. Sir Frederick Browning (1896–1965). He looked even younger than he was.

Boycs: see CRICKETERS.

Boy David: see 'PRIVATE EYE' NICKNAMES.

Boy George: see POP STARS.

Boy Orator of the Platitude, the: see *the Man on the Wedding Cake*.

Boy Orator of the Platte, the: (sometimes just the **Boy Orator**) William Jennings Bryan (1860–1925), the powerful speechmaker who entered the US House of Representatives in 1891 (aged 31), representing Nebraska's Platte River region. His most noted speech was the 'Cross of Gold' oration which won him the Democratic nomination in 1896. Like others, he was also known as **the Great Commoner** because of his respect for plain people whose affection he never lost. He founded a political weekly called the *Commoner* in 1901.

Bozzy: Dr Johnson's playful name for James Boswell (1740–95), his friend and biographer. Bozzy's fame rested almost entirely on his *Life of Johnson*, first published in 1791, until the discovery of his journals and papers and their publication from 1950 on.

Brandy Nan: Queen Anne (1665–1714), presumably because she was fond of it. She liked to call herself 'Mrs Morley' when she gossiped with Sarah Churchill, Duchess of Marlborough, who took the pseudonym of 'Mrs Freeman' and was nicknamed by courtiers *Queen Sarah* because of her influence. Her Scottish doctor, John Arbuthnot (1667–1735), nicknamed her **Mrs Bull**. He was also a writer of pamphlets against France and these were published as a book entitled *The History of John Bull*, 1727.

The Queen's consort, Prince George of Denmark, was given the sarcastic nickname in court circles of **Est-il Possible!** because this was his favourite remark when confronted with bad news.

Brazilian Bombshell, the: see FILM STARS.

Brenda: see 'PRIVATE EYE' NICKNAMES.

Brewer, the: see *Nosey*.

Brian: see 'PRIVATE EYE' NICKNAMES.

bright young things: young socialites of the 1920s and early 1930s whose reaction to the rigours of the recent war was to give parties and dance away the night, copied in more modest style by their poorer contemporaries. It was a short period of frivolity, disregarding the poverty and unemployment around them, flouting convention. Barbara Cartland in *We Danced All Night* (Hutchinson, 1970) called them 'bright young people' and described their noisy parties and harmless hoaxes: 'Then the young really gave the newspapers something to write about.' But, she went on, 'a very different type of people began to give parties . . . and so the idea, which at the beginning had been gay and amusing, simple and light-hearted, degenerated into something sordid and unpleasant.'

Brilliantine: see 'PRIVATE EYE' NICKNAMES.

Bristol Boy, the: Thomas Chatterton (1752−70), talented young poet who began writing verse when he was ten and in his short life produced some remarkable work, including his so-called discovery of ancient prose and poems, later proved a fake, but attractive nevertheless. He committed suicide by poison in a London garret.

Bristol Butcher, the: see BOXERS.

British Solomon, the: James I (1566–1625), an honorific matched only by the sycophantic dedication to him of the 'authorised version' of the Bible – 'Your very name is precious . . . the zeal of Your Majesty towards the house of God doth not slack . . . manifesting itself abroad in the farthest parts of Christendom . . . ' The nickname referred to his writings, including his *Daemonologie*, a denunciation of witchcraft, and it contrasted sharply with another one, **the Wisest Fool in Christendom**.

Brockton Blockbuster, the: see BOXERS.

Brown Bomber, the: see BOXERS.

Brown Eminence, the: see *l'Eminence Grise*.

Brown-jobs: see *Bluejackets*.

brownshirts: civilian army formed by Adolf Hitler and which visitors to Germany from the early 1930s found in towns and city streets, and marching and drilling in the countryside, wearing a uniform of brown shirt with swastika armband, and breeches.

Brylcreem Boys, the: young RAF officers in the early part of the Second World War, especially those who had joined the RAFVR, facetiously given this nickname (mainly by soldiers) because one such was pictured in advertisements for a popular brand of hair cream (with this name and spelling).

BTL: see GOSSIP COLUMN NICKNAMES.

Bubbles: (1) Beverly Sills (b.1929), American soprano. 'I was born with a big spit bubble in my mouth,' Miss Sills explains, 'and the doctor said "You've got to call this child Bubbles."' She adds: 'Even the Mayor (of New York) calls me "Bubbles".'
(2) Lady Rothermere. See GOSSIP COLUMN NICKNAMES.

Bubonic Plagiarist, the: see 'PRIVATE EYE' NICKNAMES.

Bubs: see *Bennies.*

Buffalo Bill: William Frederick Cody (1846—1917), American showman who took the name from his days as a buffalo hunter. In one eighteen-month period he killed 5,000 buffalo to provide meat for workers on the Kansas Pacific Railroad. His adventurous life began as a rider in the Pony Express mail service. He became a scout and guide for the US army, then served with the Kansas cavalry in the Civil War, later taking part in the Indian wars and killing the Cheyenne chief Yellow Hand in single combat. He organised his first 'wild west show' in 1883, with cowboys and Indians, and brought it to England in 1887 with spectacular success.

He was given his nickname in 1869 by his friend Ned Buntline who made him the hero of a series of dime novels and persuaded him to start his stage career.

Building Bess: Elizabeth, Countess of Shrewsbury (1520—1608), known also as **Bess of Hardwick**, a formidable lady who married four times and used her inheritance for building great houses in Derbyshire and elsewhere, including Hardwick Hall and the completion of Chatsworth, seats of the later Dukes of Devonshire. Legend says that she felt she would die if she wasn't building something.

Bullfrog of the Pontine Marshes, the: Benito Mussolini (1883—1945), thus derisively named by Winston Churchill in the Second World War.

Bull Moose, the: Theodore Roosevelt (1858—1919), 26th US President (1901—9), attempted to re-enter politics in 1912. 'I am as strong as a bull moose,' he had reassured a supporter in 1900 when running for Vice-President. The nickname was applied to him and to the Progressive 'Bull Moose' Party. Earlier he had been known as **Rough Rider** because he had helped organise and lead the First Regiment of US Cavalry Volunteers, known as Rough Riders, in the Spanish-American War (1898). Returning from that engagement as something of a hero he was called **the Man on**

Horseback. His interventionist policies when President led to his being known as **Teddy the Meddler**.

Bunny: Robertson Hare (1891–1979), the comedy actor – an inevitable nickname for anyone called Hare. Perhaps more frequently an inseparable for people called Warren. (It was also, incidentally, Jackie Kennedy's pet name for her husband, President John F. Kennedy.)

Burlington Harry: Henry Flitcroft (1697–1769), eminent architect whose patron was Lord Burlington for whom he designed Burlington House in London. He worked on other great houses and designed London churches.

Busby's Babes: younger members of Manchester United football team whose manager, Matt (later Sir Matthew) Busby, coached into a new winning side after the loss of experienced players in an air crash at Munich, 1958.

Buster: A general US nickname given to a boy but often continuing in use long after, e.g. 'Buster' Keaton, the film comedian, was christened Joseph Francis, and 'Buster' Crabbe, the swimming champion and 1930s film star was born Clarence Linden.

Butch: A general US nickname which has only recently acquired the connotations of the adjectival 'butch' meaning exaggeratedly masculine. Robert Le Roy Parker (1886–1909) and Harry Longbaugh (*c*.1860–1909) were the real names of the turn of the century outlaws known as **Butch Cassidy** and **the Sundance Kid**. Parker/Cassidy was called 'Butch' because he had once been a butcher. Longbaugh had once carried out a daring bank raid in the town of Sundance, Nevada.

Butcher, the: Ulysses S. Grant (1822–85), commander-in-chief of Union forces in the American Civil War and 18th President of the USA (1869–77). His opponents in the North called him this because they thought he was careless of the lives of men in his army. Also known as **Old Three Stars** and **the American Sphinx** (because he was uncommunicative and enigmatic). **Unconditional Surrender** (matching his initials US) evoked the first major Union victory over the Confederates when he declared 'no terms except unconditional surrender' to a Confederate general who had asked for the best terms of capitulation. Critics opposed to his running for a third term and his tyrannical ways called him **American Caesar**.

Butcher of Broadway, the: Alexander Woollcott (1887–1943), noted and feared drama critic in New York.

Butcher of Culloden, the: the Duke of Cumberland, second son of George II, who ruthlessly suppressed the Jacobites and defeated them with great slaughter at the Battle of Culloden, 1746.

Butcher of Lyons, the: Klaus Barbie (b.1913), head of the German Gestapo in Lyons from 1942 to 1944, so called because of his alleged cruelty, torture and murder of French Resistance fighters and others. He is said to have ordered the execution of more than 4,000 people and the deportation of 7,000 French Jews to concentration camps. Twice tried *in absentia*, Barbie was brought back to Lyons from exile in Bolivia in 1983 and tried again.

Similarly, General Gholam Ali Oveissi was known as **the Butcher of Tehran**. Under the Shah of Iran, he earned the lasting hatred of the Ayatollah Khomeini's followers when he ordered troops to open fire on protest marches, first in 1963 and then again in 1978. He was himself shot dead in 1984.

Butler: see FILM STARS.

C

Cad, the: see GOSSIP COLUMN NICKNAMES.

Cairo Fred: see FILM STARS.

Calamity Jane: Martha Jane Canary (1852–1903) of Deadwood, South Dakota, behaved like a cowboy but was generally unlucky in nefarious activities and brought catastrophe on her associates. Eleven of her twelve husbands died untimely deaths. She claimed to have been an Indian scout and pony-express rider. She dressed, swore and shot like a man, and eventually went into show business. Doris Day portrayed her in a 1953 film biography. 'Calamity Jane' became a common nickname for female prophets of doom, but this does not reflect the nature of Mary Jane Canary. What she did was to threaten 'calamity' to any man who offended her.

Camelot: members of John F. Kennedy's administration 1961 to 1963 plus hangers-on. In January 1961, the inauguration of a stylish, young US President, with glamorous wife at his side, aroused hopes of better things to come, following the sober Eisenhower years. The nickname, evoking the romantic idea of knights in shining armour, arose because the Lerner - Loewe musical, *Camelot*, depicting Arthur and Guinevere's court, had opened on Broadway in December 1960.

Capability Brown: Lancelot Brown (1715–83), architect and landscape gardener, noted for planning a naturalistic type of garden for the great houses of England, with vistas of trees, lakes and flower-beds. His usual comment after carrying out a survey was, 'It's capable' or 'It has capabilities.'

Captain Bob: see GOSSIP COLUMN NICKNAMES.

cardigan: one of several eponymous nicknames for wearing apparel which commemorate a personality, this one the 7th Earl of Cardigan who led the Light Brigade in the famous and disastrous charge at Balaclava in the Crimean War, 1854. Lord Cardigan gave his name to the knitted woollen jacket, or waistcoat with or without sleeves, which soldiers wore against the intense cold of the Russian winter (the battle itself gave the name 'balaclava' to the woollen cap which enveloped the head). His Lordship was not always so brave: see *the Noble Yachtsman*.

Casanova: a promiscuous lover, as was Casanova de Seingalt (1725–98), Italian adventurer and philanderer, who boasted of his conquests, which he recounted in an auto-biography. He was a supreme 'con man' of many talents, frequenting the courts and aristocratic homes of Europe.

Cassandra: a prophet of doom, hence a pessimist, the proto-type being Cassandra, daughter of Priam and Hecuba in Greek legend, who often foretold disaster; but Apollo (whom she had rejected) arranged that nobody believed her.

Cat's Eyes: Group Capt. John Cunningham (b.1917), distin-guished RAF night fighter pilot in the Second World War. Even when navigational aids were not available he man-aged to shoot down some twelve German aircraft.

Cavaliers: Royalists supporting Charles I in his struggle with the Parliamentarians (whom they dubbed *Roundheads*). Antonia Fraser in *Cromwell: Our Chief of Men* explains that the origin was the Spanish *caballeros* 'and mocked the alleged allegiance of the English court to foreign Catholic ways'.

Chairman of the Board, the: see *the Gov'nor*.

Champion, the: see *the Grand Old Man*.

Charlie: see *vandyke*.

Charlies: night watchmen, from the seventeenth century, probably because it was under Charles I that a system of policing the streets was regularised.

Charlie's Aunt: see 'PRIVATE EYE' NICKNAMES.

Cheeky Chappie, the: see SHOW BUSINESS STARS.

Cheryl: see 'PRIVATE EYE' NICKNAMES.

Chicago 7, the: people charged with creating disorder during the Democratic Convention at Chicago in 1966. Although, previously, there had been **the Hollywood 10** (blacklisted film people protesting against McCarthyite investigations in 1947 and refusing to tell the Unamerican Activities Committee whether or not they were communists), it was the label applied by the press and by their supporters to the Chicago group that set a pattern for nicknaming protesters who had run up against the law. In the USA there followed **the Wilmington 10;** in the UK, **the Pentonville 5, the Clay Cross 6, the Stockport 6,** and many more. Almost invariably accompanied by 'Free the . . .' to make a slogan.

Chief, the: Herbert Hoover (1874–1964), 31st US President (1929–33), attracted this name, in particular, although it is an inevitable one for any boss or president. Hoover was given the name because of the influence he exerted as Secretary of Commerce, 1917–21. The US President is traditionally greeted with the music of 'Hail to the Chief'.

Chindits, the: a Long-Range Penetration Force, commanded by Major-General Orde Wingate, operating behind the Japanese lines in Burma in the Second World War, making long marches or landing in gliders. These troops, carrying out daring raids, adopted a Burmese dragon-like device – the *chinthe* – as their emblem. When Churchill reported their exploits to the American President, Roosevelt described them as 'an epic achievement for the airborne troops, not forgetting the mules'.

Chinese Gordon: General Charles George Gordon (1833–85) who commanded a Chinese contingent (with Western officers) in the army of the Chinese emperor during the Tai-Ping rebellion of 1851–64. He was honoured with the rank of mandarin, first class, but refused presents of money. He became governor of the Egyptian Sudan from 1877 to 1880, and four years later returned to organise an Egyptian withdrawal from the fierce Mahdi rebellion. He defended Khartoum for nearly a year, but was killed on the steps of his fortified residence, two days before the arrival of a relief force.

Chips: Sir Henry Channon (1897—1958), American-born Conservative MP, London society figure and diarist. Robert Rhodes James, editing the diaries (Weidenfeld, 1967), wrote: 'Henry Channon III was always called "Chips" by his European friends. No one has been able to explain exactly how he acquired the sobriquet. One suggestion was that he introduced potato chips as cocktail party fare to London. Another version — considerably more plausible — was that he once shared a bachelor house with a friend known as "Fish".'

Chubby Checker: see POP STARS.

Chug: Admiral of the Fleet Sir Arthur Knyvet Wilson VC (1842—1921) was nicknamed 'Chug'. Churchill observed that this was because he was 'always working i.e. pulling, hauling, tugging'. From the phonetic distortion of 'Chug' comes the inevitable nickname 'Tug' applied to anybody called Wilson. This one was also known as **Old 'Ard 'Art**.

Clay Cross 6, the: see *the Chicago 7.*

clippie: bus conductress, mainly in London and the big cities, who took over the clipping of tickets from male conductors in the Second World War. It continued as a woman's occupation for many years.

Cliveden Set, the: writers, journalists and politicians invited to weekend parties at Cliveden, the Buckinghamshire home of Lord and Lady Astor during the 1930s. Some were alleged to be in favour of appeasement with Nazi Germany. The name was invented by Claud Cockburn's publication *The Week.*

Clothes Horse, the: see FILM STARS.

Clown Prince of Wales, the: see SHOW BUSINESS STARS.

Coachie: see *Billy Blue*.

cockneys: traditionally, those Londoners born within sound of Bow bells (St Mary-le-Bow), Cheapside,and distinctive in speech and customs. The nickname has been used since the seventeenth century but the word goes back to the Latin *coquina*, kitchen, as the cockneys were either 'servants of the kitchen' or addicted to a soft life. Hence, the old nickname 'cockney' for an effeminate person, pampered by city life. It is allied to the fabled Land of Cockaigne (kitchenland), supposedly filled with sensual delights. A thirteenth-century satire on monks who enjoyed their food and wine at the expense of spiritual devotion tells of them living in this 'land ihote Cokaygne . . . Thogh paradis be miri and bright, Cokaygne is of fairir sight'.

Cock of the North, the: George, 5th Duke of Gordon (1770–1836) who raised the regiment, the Gordon Highlanders, in 1795 and which he commanded in Spain and elsewhere.

Cold War Witch: see *the Iron Lady*.

Colossus of (American) Independence, the: John Adams (1735–1826), 2nd President of the USA (1797–1801), who helped draft the Declaration of Independence and, as Thomas Jefferson remarked, was 'the pillar of support' in the debate on its adoption. Also known as **the Colossus of Debate** and **the Machiavelli of Massachusetts**.

Conkey: see *the Iron Duke*.

Contemptibles: see *the Old Contemptibles*.

Cook's Tour: an extensive tour, after Thomas Cook (1808–92), the pioneer of tourism and founder of the firm still bearing his name.

Copper Nose: see *Nosey*.

Cordobes, El: professional name of Manuel Benitez (b.*c*.1936), leading Spanish bull-fighter. The name means 'man from Cordoba'.

Corgi and Bess: broadcasting nickname for the Christmas message given annually on radio and TV by HM Queen Elizabeth II (noted for her canine pets).

cotquean: an effeminate man. No. 482 of *The Spectator*, 1712, contains a letter supposedly written by a wife about the type of man:

> who, in several parts of England, goes by the name of 'cotquean'. I have misfortune to be joined for life with one of this character, who in reality is more of a woman than I am. He was bred up under the tuition of a tender mother, till she made him as good a housewife as herself . . . He has the whitest hand that you ever saw in your life, and raises paste better than any woman in England. These qualifications make him a sad husband.

Count Basie: see JAZZ MUSICIANS.

Count Dracula: see GOSSIP COLUMN NICKNAMES.

Crafty Cook, the: see *the Galloping Gourmet*.

CRICKETERS: As is demonstrated annually by Ian Sproat's *The Cricketers' Who's Who*, there are few leading cricketers who do not acquire a nickname at some time, even if only a simple diminutive. For example, of players prominent at the time of writing:

Ian Botham is known as **Guy the Gorilla**
Geoffrey Boycott is known as **Fiery**, **Boycs** and **Thatch**
Basil D'Oliveira is known as **Doddles**
and Keith Fletcher is known as **the Gnome**.

Freddie Trueman has long been known to the public at large

as **Fiery Fred** and commentator Don Mosey as **the Alderman.** See also *the Grand Old Man* and *Ranji*.

Crookback: see *the Boar*.

Crouchback: Edmund, Earl of Lancaster (1245−96), second son of Henry III, perhaps for the same reason as 'Crookback'.

Crum-hell: see *Nosey*.

Cry Guy, the: see POP STARS.

Cuddles: see FILM STARS.

Cuddly Ken: see DISC JOCKEYS.

Cumberland Poets: see *Lake Poets*.

Curthose: Robert II, Duke of Normandy (1087−1134), elder son of William the Conqueror. In modern parlance the nickname might be 'short socks', and it referred not so much to the way he dressed but because he was a fairly small man. This is indicated by a less familiar nickname, **Short-thigh**.

Curtmantle: Henry II (1133−89), first of the Plantagenets, who introduced a shorter coat or smock than was customary in the English court, perhaps because it was a more convenient garb for hunting, to which he was addicted. It was also called the 'Anjou mantle', Henry being Count of Anjou where the fashion originated. Previously the English nobles wore robes to the ankle, whereas the Anjou style ended at the knees.

D

Dad's Army: the Local Defence Volunteers (LDV) formed in Britain at the outbreak of the Second World War, soon renamed the Home Guard; a posthumous nickname given by those looking back on the exploits of this civilian (though uniformed and attached to army units) force, many of whom were elderly men. A long-running BBC television series (from 1968) under this title established the nickname with affectionate humour.

dagmars: bullet shapes on the front bumpers of American cars during the 1950s. They were named after a well-endowed actress, Jennie Lewis, known as Dagmar, who appeared on TV comedy shows.

Dame Harold: see 'PRIVATE EYE' NICKNAMES.

Dancing Chancellor, the: Sir Christopher Hatton (1540–91), Chancellor of England and favourite of Elizabeth I, noted for his grace and skill in dancing, especially in the galliard which the queen so much enjoyed. 'That Hatton was an accomplished dancer and a skilled performer in the tilt-yard is true enough. But a study of his life dispels the legend that he owed his astonishing progress from an obscure country squire to a dazzling position, with the Woolsack as crowning achievement, to such adventitious graces' (Eric St John Brooks, *Sir Christopher Hatton*, Cape, 1946).

Dancing Divinity, the: see FILM STARS.

Danny the Red: (sometimes **Red Dany**) Daniel Cohn-Bendit (b.1945), a leading figure in the 1968 student uprising in France. A West German, he was studying at Nanterre University. By way of reference to a female impersonator becoming popular at the time he was also dubbed (in Britain) **Danny le Rouge**.

Darby and Joan: an old couple, happy in their long marriage, in modest but contented circumstances. A ballad on this theme was published in 1735. Whether it was inspired by two such estimable people is not known, but one tradition is that there was a London couple of that name, another that they lived in West Yorkshire.

Dark Horse (President), the: James A. Garfield (1831−81), 20th US President (1881). He won the Republican nomination as a compromise candidate in 1880. He was assassinated. (A nickname also applied to many unexpected candidates for the Presidency − see *the Fraud* and *Young Hickory*.)

Dark Lady of the Sonnets, the: the beauty to whom Shakespeare addressed some of his Sonnets (from cxxvii on) − her eyes were 'raven black' and so was her hair − and she figures in some of the plays. Her identity has been a subject for literary detectives for many years, and the candidates are numerous. A.L.Rowse is convinced he has discovered who she was − the wife of a court musician and former mistress of the Lord Chamberlain (see his *Shakespeare the Man*, Macmillan, 1973).

Darling of the Halls, the: see SHOW BUSINESS STARS.

Daubaway Weirdsley: see *Awfully Weirdly*.

Deep Throat: the anonymous source within the Nixon White House who fed *Washington Post* journalists Carl Bernstein and Bob Woodward with information which helped in their Watergate investigations (1972−4). It has been suggested that 'Deep Throat' never existed but was a cover for unjustified suppositions. However, the reporters explained:

> Woodward had promised he would never identify him or his position to anyone . . . In newspaper terminology, this meant the discussions were on 'deep background' . . . Woodward explained the arrangement to managing editor Howard Simons one day. He had taken to calling the source 'my friend', but Simons dubbed him Deep

Throat, the title of a celebrated pornographic movie (*All The President's Men*, Secker & Warburg, 1974).

Desert Fox, the: Field Marshal Erwin Rommel (1891–1944), noted for his audacious generalship in North Africa during the Second World War.

Desert Rats, the: the British 7th Armoured Division which served throughout the North Africa campaign in the Second World War and adopted the badge of a desert rat (the jerboa). The division made use of 'scurrying and biting' tactics in desert warfare and later fought in the invasion of occupied Europe, from Normandy onwards.

Dictionary Johnson: Dr Samuel Johnson (1709–84) because of his *Dictionary of the English Language*, 1755 – 'and it should not pass unobserved that he has quoted no author whose writings had a tendency to hurt sound religion and morality', says Boswell in his *Life*. He addressed the 'plan' for the dictionary to the Earl of Chesterfield ('a nobleman who was very ambitious of literary distinction') and worked three years on it, employing six secretaries. The work is notable for its definitions and citations and amounts to the first authoritative English dictionary. Boswell records that 'the reward of his labour was only fifteen hundred and seventy-five pounds; and when the expense of amanuenses and paper, and other articles, are deducted, his clear profit was very inconsiderable'.

Tobias George Smollett, Johnson's contemporary, dubbed him **the Great Cham (of Literature)** in a letter to John Wilkes, 1759. 'Cham' is a form of 'khan' – as in Genghis Khan – meaning 'monarch' or 'prince'. Other names for the learned gentleman were **the Great Moralist, the English Socrates** and – because he was a great bear of a man – **Ursa Major** (bestowed by Boswell's father).

Diddy (David): see DISC JOCKEYS.

Digger, the: see 'PRIVATE EYE' NICKNAMES.

Dirty Dai: see GOSSIP COLUMN NICKNAMES.

Dirty Digger, the: see 'PRIVATE EYE' NICKNAMES.

DISC JOCKEYS: radio presenters of popular music on records, linking these with commentary. Such 'jockeys' became personalities in their own right from the 1950s, each with a distinctive style. Some, in turn, have acquired their own nicknames:

> **Cuddly Ken:** Kenny Everett (b.1944). Probably self-applied, *c*.1973, when promoting Capital Radio — also alliteratively described as 'Cuddly Capital'.
> **Diddy David:** David Hamilton (b.1939). Of diminutive proportions, he was given the name when appearing in TV shows of the 1960s with the Liverpool comedian, Ken Dodd. Dodd had already begun to popularise the Scouse adjective for small, 'diddy', in connection with leprechaun-like characters he called 'Diddymen'. 'Diddy Uncle Jack' was how the family used to describe Dodd's great-uncle. He now uses the word, he says, to describe anything 'quaint, small and lovable', which may or may not apply to David Hamilton.
> 'Diddy' was also the family pet-name of Thomas Creevey (1768–1838), the Liverpool-born MP and diarist.
> **Fluff:** Alan Freeman (b.*c*.1927), Australian disc jockey, working in Britain. Unkind people might think the name stuck because of a propensity for verbal errors, but not according to the man himself: 'No! It was an old, old pullover of mine that I had dry-cleaned. It made it so incredibly fluffy that I got introduced at a party as Fluff Freeman and the name stuck'.
> **Living Legend, the:** Tony Blackburn (b.1943), the first voice heard on BBC Radio 1 in 1967.
> **Stewpot:** Ed Stewart (b.1941), from the traditional schoolboy name for a 'swot' or 'swotpot' — one who works studiously. Not applied until he was in his twenties. Inappropriate then, so ironic.

Divine Callas, the: Maria Callas (1923–77), American/Greek prima donna who began her career in Italy. Other versions include: **La Divina, La Diva, La Callas** — the latter form of 'La' + surname being the traditional way of denoting female opera singers (or other women of a grand or temperamental nature).

Divine Sarah, the: Sarah Bernhardt (1844–1923), the great French tragic actress.

Dixie: William R. Dean (1907–80), popular footballer of the 1920s and 30s. In the 1927–8 season he set a First Division record by scoring sixty goals. He hated the nickname, preferring 'Bill'. 'Dixie', however, became an inseparable nickname for any man named Dean.

Dizzy: (1) Benjamin Disraeli, 1st Earl of Beaconsfield (1804–81), politician and novelist. He held the offices of Chancellor of the Exchequer and Prime Minister, and was creator of the Conservative Party. He became a trusted friend of Queen Victoria. The nickname, drawn from his name, was regarded as particularly apt because in his early career he was flamboyant in manner and dress. His first speech in the House of Commons in 1837 was ridiculed. He lost his temper at the laughter and interruptions, and (according to the historian Justin McCarthy) he raised his hands 'and opening his mouth as widely as its dimensions would admit, said in a remarkably loud and almost terrific tone: "I have begun several times many things, and I have often succeeded at last. Ay, Sir, and though I sit down now, the time will come when you will hear me!"' Thence a nickname applied to any clever man.
    (2) Jay Hanna 'Dizzy' Dean (1911–74), American baseball player and commentator. His name derived from a comment by a coach at a game in Houston: 'That kid makes you look dizzy.'
    (3) 'Dizzy' Gillespie. see JAZZ MUSICIANS.

Django: see JAZZ MUSICIANS.

Dockers' KC, the: Ernest Bevin (1881–1951) who became Minister of Labour and National Service during the Second World War and held other high offices. The nickname was given him by the press when he was national organiser of the dockers' union, 1910–21. In 1920 he presented demands for better wages and conditions to a commission of inquiry. (KC = King's Counsel.)

Doctor, the: see 'PRIVATE EYE' NICKNAMES.

Doctor Subtilis: John Duns Scotus (*c.*1266—1308), philosopher and theologian, whose skill in debate earned him this nickname meaning 'cunning teacher'. He defended the papacy against the theory of the divine right of kings. His followers were ridiculed and nicknamed **Duns,** which grew into the word 'dunce', one who is dull-witted or slow to learn.

Doddles: see CRICKETERS.

Dolly Varden: a youthful style of flowered print dress, slim-waisted, and with flower-bedecked hat worn coquettishly tilted on the head, or a wide-brimmed hat with small crown and tied with ribbon under the chin, as in early illustrations of Dickens's *Barnaby Rudge* (1840) where she appears and his description of this simple, gay and pretty girl. The affectionate nickname — 'She's a regular Dolly Varden' — was current from mid-Victorian times. Dickens described the locksmith's daughter as a madcap with a roguish face, 'a face lighted up by the loveliest pair of sparkling eyes . . . the face of a pretty, laughing girl; dimpled and fresh, and healthful — the very impersonation of good-humour and blooming beauty'.

Don Giovanni: a handsome and unscrupulous heart-breaker, another name for Don Juan, as in Mozart's opera. Said ensign Spooney in Thackeray's *Vanity Fair:* "That Osborne's a devil of a fellow . . . and since he's been home they say he's a regular Don Giovanni, by Jove!" Stubble and Spooney thought that to be a "regular Don Giovanni, by Jove" was one of the finest qualities a man could possess.'

Don Juan: a great lover, from the legendary character whose ancestry goes further back than his first published appearance in Barcelona, 1630. This dissolute gallant — sometimes with supernatural overtones — has been the subject of books, plays and operas.

Dorcas: a kindly woman, socially conscious, and one who busies herself in practical charity; from the woman described in *Acts,* 9 (Tabitha in Aramaic, Dorcas in Greek) whom Peter brought to life when dead. 'She was full of good works and acts of charity . . . All the widows stood beside him weeping, and showing tunics and other garments which Dorcas made while she was with them.' Dorcas societies flourished in the churches of the nineteenth and early twentieth centuries, sewing and making garments for the poor.

Doubting Thomas: a suspicious person, one hard to convince; from the disciple Thomas ('the Twin') who refused to believe his companions' story of the resurrection of Jesus until he had seen for himself. The gospel of *John*, 20 tells how he saw and touched Jesus eight days later.

doughboy: American soldier, from the size and shape of uniform buttons in the Civil War, like lumps of dough. Entirely by coincidence the nickname provides a link with the soldier of feudal times whose master paid for his services (or partly) in bread, so that in Anglo-Saxon he would be called *hlafoetan,* loaf-eater; and the Roman fighting servant was *buccellarius,* biscuit-eater. Bread, and dough from which it is made, has a long connection with the soldier.

Dragon Lady: see GOSSIP COLUMN NICKNAMES.

Dr Death: see 'PRIVATE EYE' NICKNAMES.

Dries: see *Wets.*

Duchess, the: see GOSSIP COLUMN NICKNAMES.

Dude President, the: Chester A. Arthur (1830−86), 21st President of the USA (1881−5). A dude is American slang for a dapper man. For the same reason − his being well dressed, handsome and charming − he was known as **America's First Gentleman** and **First Gentleman of This Land.** His assumption of the presidency was occasioned by the assassination of James A. Garfield, hence: **His Accidency.**

Duke: (1) Edward Kennedy Ellington (1899—1974), invariably known as 'Duke' Ellington or 'The Duke' — American composer and musician. 'Duke' has been used to refer to a dapper man in the USA since the seventeenth century.

(2) John Wayne (1907—79), American film actor noted especially for his roles in Westerns. 'I got the title of Duke when I was a little boy going to school. I had a dog named Duke. He chased the fire engines, and I chased Duke, and the men used to say "Here comes little Duke with his dog."'

Dumb Prophet, the: see *the Man of Destiny*.

Dummy: Admiral of the Fleet Sir Henry Oliver (1865—1965) who was noted for his verbal economy.

Duns: see *Doctor Subtilis*.

Dutch: (1) Ronald Reagan. See *the Gipper*.

(2) HRH the Princess of Wales. An old family name short for 'the Duchess'. See also 'PRIVATE EYE' NICKNAMES.

E

Edmund Ironside: son of Ethelred 'the Unready', noted for his great strength. Edmund (*c*.980−1016), King of the West Saxons, fought valiantly against the Danish invaders until a division of England was agreed upon, he to rule the south, Canute the north.

Edward's French Lady: Julie, Madame de St Laurent, with whom Prince Edward, Duke of Kent (father of the future Queen Victoria), fourth son of George III, was said to have contracted a morganatic marriage. She was, at any rate, his close companion for more than twenty-five years before he married Mary Louise Victoria of Saxe-Coburg-Gotha.

Edward the Caresser/ the Peacemaker: see *Tum-Tum*.

Elvis the Pelvis: Elvis Presley (1935−77), internationally successful 'pop' performer with a long career, from the 1950s. The waggling of his hips in rock 'n' roll performances earned him this journalistic tag, though sometimes he was simply known as **the Pelvis.** Also: **the King of Rock 'n' Roll** or simply **the King.**

Emancipator, the: Abraham Lincoln (1809−65), 16th President of the USA (1861−5), in recognition of his emancipation of the slaves in 1863. Sometimes: **the Great Emancipator,** though chiefly this has been a posthumous term. Lincoln's first widely known nickname (from 1858) was **Honest Abe.** He was known as **the Rail Splitter** after a log he had split was presented to the Illinois Republican State Convention in 1859. He had split rails for a living as a young man. **Old Abe,** a nickname first given by friends, was taken up, mockingly, in the South and corrupted to **Ape** or **the Illinois Baboon** (referring to his appearance). Also: **the Tycoon** and **Father**

Abraham. His bad-tempered wife was known as **the She-Wolf.**

Eminence Grise, l': François Leclerc du Tremblay (1577—1638), known as Père Joseph, private secretary to Armand Jean du Plessis, Cardinal Richelieu (1585—1642), statesman and principal adviser to Louis XIII. Richelieu, known as **L'Eminence Rouge** (or Red Cardinal) virtually ruled France from 1624 till his death. Du Tremblay, dressed in grey, became known as the Grey Cardinal because — although not a cardinal — he exercised the power of one through his influence on Richelieu. Now 'éminence grise' can be applied to any shadowy figure who exercises power — or adapted, as with **the Brown Eminence** (Martin Bormann, 1900—45?, because of his *brownshirt* background).

Empress of Emotion, the: see FILM STARS.

English Socrates, the: see *Dictionary Johnson.*

English Vitruvius, the: Inigo Jones (1573—1652), architect who introduced the Palladian style to England and had great influence on the design of great houses and public buildings, as had the Roman engineer and architect Vitruvius who wrote a treatise on the subject, dedicated to the Emperor Augustus.

Est-Il Possible! see *Brandy Nan.*

Ethelred the Unready: Ethelred (or Aethelred) II (*c.*960—1016), king of the English, given the nickname not because he was tardy but because he lacked *rede*, or good counsel, the result being that he had an unhappy reign, following a policy of opportunism, buying off the Danes from time to time and ensuring peace only for short periods.

Ettrick Shepherd, the: James Hogg (1770—1835), Scottish poet, born at Ettrick in Selkirkshire, son of a shepherd and tended sheep himself, author of pleasing ballads. Sir Walter Scott gave him powerful encouragement.

F

Fab Four, the: the Beatles (1962–70), world-famous British pop group. An early nickname. 'Fab' was a vogue word of the 1960s, short for fabulous. See also *the Fifth Beatle*.

Factory King, the: Richard Oastler (1789–1861), a Yorkshireman who campaigned against conditions of child labour in the mills, arousing public opinion. He had a leading part in the agitation which produced the ten hours bill and the passing of factory acts. While in the Fleet prison for debt he published the weekly *Fleet Papers* in which factory and poor law questions were raised.

Fair Maid of Kent, the: Joan, wife of the Black Prince — her second husband — and only daughter of Edmund Plantagenet, Earl of Kent. (Several women in history have been nicknamed 'Fair', as have kings, usually because of their hair colouring or light complexion.)

Fair Perdita: Mary Darby Robinson (1758–1800), actress and something of a writer and poet, because of her distinction as Perdita in Shakespeare's *The Winter's Tale*. When she became mistress of the Prince of Wales (later Prince Regent and George IV) — who called himself her **Florizel** (in the play, Prince of Bohemia) — they wrote to each other in these names. Later she was mistress of Charles James Fox, the statesman, but she died in poverty.

Fargo Express, the: see BOXERS.

Farmer George: George III (1738–1820), one of whose interests outside politics was agriculture. When Arthur Young, writer and pioneer of scientific farming, issued his *Annals of Agriculture*, the King contributed information about his farm at Petersham under the name of Ralph Robinson.

Fatha: see JAZZ MUSICIANS.

Father Abraham: see *the Emancipator*.

Father of His Country, the: George Washington (1732–99), 1st President of the USA (1789–97). First used on a 1778 calendar, published in Pennsylvania, in German: 'Das Landes Vater'. Also known as **the American Cincinnatus** – because like the fifth century BC Roman hero he had left his farm to serve his country – and **the American Fabius.** His critics riposted with: **the Old Fox** (because of his cunning) and **the Stepfather of His Country** (implying that he took over another's duties or position).

Father of the Constitution, the: James Madison (1751–1836), 4th President of the USA (1809–17). He helped to draft the Constitution and the Bill of Rights.

Fats: (1) Fats Waller. See JAZZ MUSICIANS.
(2) Fats Domino. See POP STARS.

Fatty: (1) Roscoe Arbuckle (1887–1933), silent comedy star whose career ended with a scandal in 1921. In *The Lore and Language of Schoolchildren* (1959), Iona and Peter Opie reveal how they discovered that the names 'Fatty Harbuckle', 'Fatty Harbottle', 'Fatty Arbicle' and 'Fatty Artabuckles' were a common way of describing fat people, even though the children who used these names had no idea of their origin.
(2) Lord Soames. See 'PRIVATE EYE' NICKNAMES.

Feather-Duster of Dutchess County, the: see *the Boss*.

Female Howard, the: Elizabeth Fry (1780–1845), the Quaker prison reformer, because she followed in the steps of John Howard (1726–90), a pioneer in this branch of philanthropy. Like Howard, Elizabeth Fry was appalled at prison conditions and she devoted her life to improving them, with special attention to women prisoners. Like Howard, too, she visited prisons abroad as well as in Britain.

Few, the: fighter pilots of the RAF at the height of the

German air attacks on London and the south-east of England in 1940. Although greatly outnumbered they wreaked havoc on the Luftwaffe, with heavy losses to themselves. Paying tribute to these airmen who were 'undaunted by odds, unwearied in their constant challenge and mortal danger', Winston Churchill, Prime Minister, said in the House of Commons, 20 August 1940: 'Never in the field of human conflict was so much owed by so many to so few.'

Fiddle and the Bow, the: see FILM STARS.

Fiery Fred: see CRICKETERS.

Fifth Beatle, the: Brian Epstein (1934–67), the group's manager, was so dubbed — much to his annoyance — by Murray the K, an American disc jockey, in 1964. Others could more fittingly have merited the title — Stu Sutcliffe, an early member of the group who was eased out and died before fame struck, and Neil Aspinall, road manager, aide and friend. The phrase is sometimes applied to other people who miss out on the success of something they have once been a part of.

Fifth Estate, the: see *the Fourth Estate*.

Fighting Marine, the: see BOXERS.

FILM STARS: Few film stars have been given nicknames by their fans. They have either arisen within the film industry or have been applied as promotional labels, chiefly the latter. A selection:

> **America's Boy Friend:** Charles 'Buddy' Rogers. Light leading man of the 1920s and 30s.
> **America's Sweetheart:** see *the World's Sweetheart* below.
> **Anatomic Bomb, the:** Silvana Pampanini.
> **Beard, the:** Monty Woolley, ebullient character actor, from the late 1930s onwards.
> **Biograph Girl, the:** Florence Lawrence, silent screen star.
> **Body, the:** Marie McDonald, former model.
> **Bogey:** Humphrey Bogart.
> **Brazilian Bombshell, the:** Carmen Miranda, Portuguese singer, often dressed like a fruit salad.

Butler: Sir Richard Attenborough (because he looks and behaves like an old retainer?).

Cairo Fred: Omar Sharif, world-weary Egyptian.

Clothes Horse, the: Joan Crawford, who frequently 'suffered in mink'.

Cuddles: S.Z. Sakall, Hungarian comic character actor.

Dancing Divinity, the: Jessie Matthews, British star of 1930s musicals.

Duke: John Wayne. See sep. entry.

Empress of Emotion, the: Elissa Landi, Austrian-Italian leading lady of the 1930s.

Fatty: Roscoe Arbuckle. See sep. entry.

Fiddle and the Bow, the: Laurel and Hardy.

First Gentleman of the Screen, the: George Arliss, old-style British actor who usually played kings, statesmen, etc.

First Lady of the Screen, the: Norma Shearer, American star of the 1920s and 30s.

Great Profile, the: see *the World's Greatest Actor* below.

Handsomest Man in the World, the: Francis X. Bushman, hefty American silent film star.

Hockey Stick, the: Julie Andrews — because she is very 'British' and thus may have some of the attributes of the hockey-player, chin up, and all that. Cf. the traditional girls' private school exclamation: 'Jolly hockey sticks!'

Iron Butterfly, the: Jeanette Macdonald. Also limited application to Julie Andrews.

It Girl, the: see sep. entry.

Kid, the: Warren Beatty, known as such to close friends and to his big sister, Shirley Maclaine.

King of Hollywood, the: Clark Gable, American star whose career spanned thirty years.

King of the Cowboys, the: Tom Mix, first, then Roy Rogers.

King of the Serials, the: Buster Crabbe, best known as the original Flash Gordon and Buck Rogers in 1930s film serials. See also *Buster*.

Lolla, La: Gina Lollobrigida.

Love Rouser, the: Buddy Rogers (in 1928). See also *America's Boy Friend* above.

Magnificent Wildcat, the: Pola Negri, Polish-born star of the silent screen.

Man of a Thousand Faces, the: Lon Chaney senior (a master of make-up).

Man You Love To Hate, the: Erich von Stroheim, Austrian-born portrayer of villains.

Master, the: see sep. entry.

One-Take: see sep. entry.

Oomph Girl, the: Ann Sheridan, former beauty contest winner.

Peekaboo Girl, the: Veronica Lake (her hair-do covered one eye).

Platinum Blonde, the: Jean Harlow. Coined by Howard Hughes on account of her almost white hair.

Screen's Master Character Actor, the: Lon Chaney junior.

Sex Kitten, the: Brigitte Bardot.

Sex Thimble, the: Dudley Moore (a mere 5 feet 2½ inches).

Sexy Rexy: Rex Harrison, much-married old English smoothy.

Singing Capon, the: Nelson Eddy.

Sweater Girl, the: Lana Turner.

Threat, the: Lizabeth Scott, sultry 1940s leading lady.

Viennese Teardrop, the: Luise Rainer, Austrian-born actress.

World's Greatest Actor, the: John Barrymore (especially for *Don Juan*, 1927). See *the Great Profile* above.

World's Greatest Actress, the: Marie Dressler, silent comedy star.

World's Sweetheart, the: Mary Pickford. She began her career as a child actress and progressed to such popularity in the cinema that the honorific **America's Sweetheart** had to be enlarged. So shrewd was she at business that the nickname **the Bank of America's Sweetheart** also stuck to her, and **Attila of Sunnybrook Farm.**

Zero: Samuel Joel Mostel was known throughout his career as 'Zero' in recognition of his scholastic achievement at Public School 188 in New York.

See also THE MARX BROTHERS.

Finest, the: New York City police, from about 1930 onwards. Later the use became ironic, as in: 'New York's finest − the best that money can buy'.

First Dark Horse, the: see *Young Hickory*.

First Gentleman of Europe, the: see *Prinny*.

First Gentleman of the Screen, the: see FILM STARS.

First Gentleman of This Land, the: see *the Dude President*.

First Lady of the Air, the: an English nickname-title for Gladys Young, distinguished radio actress who died in 1975 after a broadcasting career of nearly forty years. Her voice became familiar to millions of listeners. A *Radio Times* note to a tributary programme said: 'Her contribution to the development of radio drama is incalculable.'
(For **First Lady of the Screen, the:** see FILM STARS.)
The 'First Lady' tag is just as open to abuse as the 'First Gentleman of this and that'. One of the authors heard Esther Rantzen, the broadcaster, being introduced in 1979 as 'Britain's First Lady of Television'. Alas, it was her husband who was doing the introduction. In the USA, **the First Lady of Television** has been more fittingly applied to Lucille Ball.
'First Lady', meaning the wife of the US President or his designated hostess, is not a nickname but an unofficial title dating from 1877 when it was used about Lucy Webb Hayes in an account of the inauguration of President Hayes.

Fishing Fleet, the: girls who went out to India in search of husbands during the days of the British Raj. If they were unsuccessful they were known as **Returned Empties.**

Five New Pence: see GOSSIP COLUMN NICKNAMES.

Flame-Haired Temptress, the: see 'PRIVATE EYE' NICK-NAMES.

Flanders Mare, the: Henry VIII's unkind nickname for his fourth wife, Anne of Cleves (1515–57). His dissatisfaction with her resulted in the annulment of their marriage a few months after it was solemnised in 1540.

flapper: originally a young girl whose plaited hair flapped up and down as she ran — flapping like the wings of a bird. Then in the early 1920s it was extended to mean a carefree, flirtatious young woman, often unconventional. In *We Danced All Night* (Hutchinson, 1970) Barbara Cartland writes: 'The modern girl after the war (1914–18) had at first enjoyed a kind of vogue. She was called a "flapper", although this before 1914 had meant an adolescent who was old enough to wear her hair tied with a large bow at the back. The war changed this, and in 1919 and 1920 a flapper was a high-spirited girl who typified the Modern Miss.'

This explanation was extended by Miss H. M. Drennan in a letter to the *Daily Telegraph*, 25 October 1975, defining the term as she knew it when a girl. 'Her badge of flapperdom, however, was in her hair, which she wore long and tied back with voluminous silk taffeta bows . . . it was these becoming winglike bows which provided the aptness of her title. She had great popularity with bachelors who could tease and mildly flirt without being expected to have matrimonial intentions.' The flapper began to lose her designation along with her hair when the 'bob' became fashionable, although the nickname persisted for some time as a convenient description for a merry, perhaps giddy, young woman. She was, at any rate — going back to the original meaning of the word — a 'bird', to use the later slang for her.

A different, and doubtful, explanation is made by R. Turner Wilcox in *The Dictionary of Costume* (Batsford, 1969) who says the word was used for a girl in short skirts, blouse or sweater, who in winter wore galoshes 'which were always unbuckled and flapping'.

Flash Harry: Sir Malcolm Sargent (1895–1967), orchestral conductor. The name is said to have originated with a BBC radio announcer after Sargent had appeared on the *Brains Trust* and was also about to be heard on the following programme. Listeners were now to be taken over to a concert conducted by him 'like a flash'. However, the nickname encapsulated his extemely debonair looks and manner — smoothed-back hair, buttonhole, gestures and all. When Sir Thomas Beecham heard that Sargent was conducting in Tokyo, he remarked, 'Ah! Flash in Japan!'

In due course, Sir Alexander Gibson (b.1926), conductor

of the Scottish National Orchestra, was dubbed **Flash Haggis.**

flashman: a swell (flashing his wealth about), also a patron of pugilism — one of The Fancy — in the eighteenth and nineteenth centuries.

Flip Wilson: see SHOW BUSINESS STARS.

Florizel: see *Prinny.*

flower people (or **children**): milder offshoot of the *hippies,* and like them originating in San Francisco in the mid-1960s. These young people carried flowers in the streets and at rallies, chanting the slogan 'Make love, not war'. They talked of 'flower power'.

Fluff: see DISC JOCKEYS.

Flying Finn, the: (1) Paavo Nurmi (1897–1973), famous Finnish runner whose nickname was earned by his successes in the 1924 Olympics in Paris.
(2) Hannu Mikkola, World Rally Champion 1983.

Flying Peacemaker, the: Henry Kissinger (b.1923), when US Secretary of State in the 1970s — so-called by the press because of his frequent journeys to world trouble spots and his 'shuttle diplomacy' in the Middle East and Africa.

Fog: Capt. Mark Phillips (b.1948), husband of Princess Anne. According to usage at Sandhurst, among Sloane Rangers and *Private Eye* readers, he is known thus 'because he's thick and wet . . . '

Foodies: see *Sloane Ranger.*

Forces' Sweetheart, the: Vera Lynn (b.1917), popular singer who entertained servicemen throughout the Second World War in concerts and on radio. Made a Dame in 1975.

Forgotten Army, the: the British Army in Malaya during the Second World War.

Former Naval Person: see *Winnie.*

Foul-Weather Jack: Admiral John Byron (1723—86), from his misfortunes at sea. Soon after he joined the navy he was wrecked off the coast of Chile, 1741, and he published an account of his experiences. He commanded the *Dolphin* on a voyage round the world (1764—6), became governor of Newfoundland and commanded the West Indian fleet.

Four-Eyed George: General George Gordon Meade (1815—72) of the American Army. Because he wore spectacles. Now a common nickname for those similarly afflicted.

Four-Letter Annie: see GOSSIP COLUMN NICKNAMES.

Fourth Estate, the: the press. Thomas Macaulay wrote (1828) concerning the House of Commons: 'The gallery in which the reporters sit has become the fourth estate of the realm' — (the others being the Lords Spiritual, the Lords Temporal and the Commons). Edmund Burke may have coined the phrase first, however. It has also been suggested that the BBC has become **the Fifth Estate.**

Fragrant Hackette, the: see GOSSIP COLUMN NICKNAMES.

Franklin Deficit Roosevelt: see *the Boss.*

Fraud, the: Rutherford B. Hayes (1822—93), 19th President of the USA (1877—81), who received fewer popular votes than his opponent in the disputed election of 1876. Hence also **the President De Facto** because supporters of his opponent, Tilden, would not concede that he was President *de jure.* Another **Dark Horse President** he was acclaimed by some as **the Hero of '77.**

Frederick the Great: see *the Philosopher of Sans-Souci.*

Free-born John: John Lilburne (*c.*1614—57), a leader of the Levellers, a Christian democratic movement during the Civil wars in England and under the Commonwealth, its members mainly from the soldiers in the Parliamentary army, urging political reforms. Lilburne referred to himself as 'an honest, true-bred, free-born Englishman'. He was high-minded but argumentative: it was said of him that if he were the only person left in the world 'Lilburne would quarrel with John, and John with Lilburne'. He suffered the pillory, imprisonment and fines for his convictions.

Fritz: Walter Mondale (b.1928), US Vice-President (1977—81). His middle name is Frederick and Fritz is the traditional German pet name for people called Friedrich. In Britain, Fritz was wartime Forces lingo for a German soldier from the First World War onwards. Mondale also earned the name **Norwegian Wood** during his bid for the presidency in 1984 because of his ancestry and stiff manner (alluding to the title of a Beatles' song).

Fruity Metcalfe: Captain Edward Metcalfe, bouncy equerry on the staff of Edward VIII, when Prince of Wales. George V considered 'Fruity' a bad influence and tried, in vain, to keep them apart. But what a jolly nickname.

Fum the Fourth: see *Prinny*.

G

Gaffer, the: Sir Basil Blackwell (1889–1984), bookseller and publisher, son of the founder of Oxford's main bookshop and responsible for its expansion. On his death, the *Bookseller* described him as 'undoubtedly the greatest book trade figure of this century, perhaps any.' Although he lived – and worked – to a ripe old age, Blackwell was already known as 'the Gaffer' in his forties. His son Richard, who predeceased him, was known as **the Gov'nor.**

Gallant Leader, the: see *the Boss.*

Galloping Dick: Richard Ferguson, one of several highwaymen whose exploits earned them nicknames. He was hanged at Aylesbury in 1800. The nickname would have been appropriate for his more famous predecessor, Dick (Richard) Turpin who met a similar fate in 1739, but it does not seem to have been applied.

Galloping Gourmet, the: Graham Kerr (b.1934), jokey, British-born cookery expert whose TV programmes were made in Canada but seen in many countries during the late 1960s and early 70s. He was known as 'galloping' because he did everything very quickly. Cf. **the Crafty Cook** – a name used by Michael Barry (Bukht), a radio and TV cookery expert from the mid-1970s, specialising in short-cut methods.

Game Chicken, the: see BOXERS.

Gang of Four, the: (1) Conspiratorial group led by Jiang Qing, unscrupulous widow of Chairman Mao Tse-tung – so labelled in the mid-1970s, when the four were tried and given the death sentence for treason and other crimes (later commuted to life imprisonment). The other three members were Zhang Chunqiao, a political organiser in the Cultural

Revolution, Wang Hogwen, a youthful activist, and Yao Wenyuan, a journalist. Chairman Hua Kuo-feng attributed the phrase to his predecessor. Apparently, on one occasion, Mao had warned his wife and her colleagues: 'Don't be a gang of four.'

(2) The founders of the British Social Democratic Party, from 1981 namely Roy Jenkins, David Owen, William Rodgers and Shirley Williams.

GANGSTERS: Whereas murderers and other noted criminals have commonly had nicknames applied to them by press or public, gangsters have given each other names. Perhaps it made them feel tougher or, in some cases, more lovable than they actually were. The following sample of names is drawn largely from US organised crime of the Capone era (for him personally, see *Scarface*) i.e. the 1920s and 30s. Almost every gangster of that period had a nickname. Often it emphasised no more than ethnic background (Theodore **The Greek** Anton), some physical defect (Charlie **Cherry Nose** Gioe) or sought just to be unpleasant (Izzy **The Rat** Buchalsky). Here are some of the more intriguingly descriptive (one does not always know why they were so called). The sobriquets are presented, in customary fashion, as part of the gangster's full name (much useful information from John Kobler's *Capone: The Life and World of Al Capone*, Putnam's 1971):

> John Joseph **Bathhouse Jim** Coughlin (he once worked as a rubber in a Turkish bath)
> **Blubber Bob** Gray (he weighed 300 pounds)
> George **Bugs** Moran (was he bug-eyed or crazy, or both?)
> Benjamin **Bugsy** Siegel (ditto)
> Murray **the Camel** Humphries (he wore a camel-hair coat)
> Peter **the Clutching Hand** Morello
> **Crane Neck** Nugent
> Giuseppe **Diamond Joe** Esposito (he wore much jewellery)
> John **Dingbat** O'Berta
> Jim **Duffy the Goat** Franche
> Ecola **the Eagle** Baldelli (from Bald Eagle?)
> Frank **the Enforcer** Nitti
> Samuel McPherson **Golf Bag** Hunt (he carried his shotgun concealed in a golf-bag)

Jake **Greasy Thumb** Guzik (described as 'porcine')
Michael **Hinky Dink** Kenna (puny sized)
Giuseppe **Hop Toad** Giunta
Joseph **Joe Bananas** Bonanno
Julius **Lovin' Putty** Annixter
Ignazio **Lupo the Wolf** Saietta
George **Machine Gun** Kelly (one of the commonest gangster 'handles', this one)
Mike de Pike Heitler (described as 'looking like a Surinam toad')
Charlie **Monkey Face** Genker (described as 'wizened')
Cornelius **Needles** Ferry (a drug addict)
Richard **Peg Leg** Lonergan
Joe **Polock Joe** Saltis (he was Polish)
Julian **Potatoes** Kaufman
Vincent **Schemer** Drucci
Orazio **the Scourge** Tropea (he had *il malocchio* − the evil eye − which he could put on people)
William Jack **Three-Fingered** White (a left-handed shot − his right hand was crushed by a brick when he was a boy)
Louis **Two-Gun** Alterie (actually he carried three)
Michael J. **Umbrella Mike** Boyle (he collected protection money in an unfurled umbrella)

(See also *Lucky*.)

garibaldi: a loose blouse worn by women in imitation of the red shirt worn by followers of Giuseppe Garibaldi, the Italian patriot (1807−82). Another example of a personal nickname for items of attire.

Gas(light)man, the: see BOXERS.

Gas 'n' Gaiters: see GOSSIP COLUMN NICKNAMES.

Gay Lothario: see *Lothario*.

Geneva Bull, the: Stephen Marshall (1594−1655), Presbyterian preacher at the time of the Commonwealth, noted for his political sermons and support of the bill for abolishing episcopacy. His delivery was loud and threatening — 'roaring like a bull' — and he followed the lead of John Calvin, theologian, who had earlier settled in Geneva and established a university there.

Gentle George: see BOXERS.

Gentle Giant, the: see BOXERS.

Gentleman Jack(son): see BOXERS.

Gentleman Jim: see BOXERS.

Gentleman Johnny: General John Burgoyne (1722–92), soldier, member of parliament and dramatist. He is remembered especially for the surrender forced upon him by the colonial troops at Saratoga in 1777, a turning-point in the American War of Independence. He returned to England amidst public indignation. His honour was later restored. He resumed his career as a witty writer of comedies. Burgoyne was somewhat vain, a bit of a dandy and man-about-town. Horace Walpole called him 'Gentleman Swagger'.

gentleman's gentleman: a valet. In fiction P.G.Wodehouse's Jeeves is the prime example. The term seems to have been first used by Sheridan in *The Rivals*, 1775.

gentlemen of the road: (1) Highwaymen. The nickname was used sarcastically in the eighteenth century as the roads became busy with stage coaches as well as horse-riders and family carriages, but stories were told of certain courtesies during robbery — a doffed hat to a lady, a wedding ring spared, a helping hand to the infirm. 'Even a highwayman, in the way of trade, may blow out your brains,' writes Hazlitt in *The Fight*, 1822, 'but if he uses foul language at the same time, I should say he was no gentleman.' Sometimes they were called **knights of the road** or **Robert's men,** from Robin Hood.

(2) Tramps have also been nicknamed thus. 'Tramps may be costing the National Health Service millions of pounds

by flitting from hospital to hospital . . Gentlemen of the road get first-class accommodation plus medical care, costing up to £100 a week or more' (*Guardian*, 21 April 1975).

Georgia Peach, the: Ty (Tyrus Raymond) Cobb (1886–1961), one of the first professional baseball players in the US. Born in Georgia, he flourished on the baseball pitch during the first three decades of the twentieth century.

GI: a self-imposed nickname for the American serviceman, much of whose supplies were marked with these initials. They may have stood for either 'Government Issue', 'Garrison Issue' or even 'Galvanised Iron'. There are many explanations. But the initials seemed appropriate to the men themselves. Their allies in the Second World War seized on the description.

Gibson girl: the young American woman, vivacious and elegant, portrayed by the American artist Charles Dana Gibson (1867–1944) and inspired by the girls of the Langhorne family into which he married. (One of his wife's sisters, Nancy, became Viscountess Astor.) His black-and-white drawings achieved tremendous popularity on both sides of the Atlantic from 1896 and well into the new century, setting a fashion in dress and hair-style as well as identifying a type of lively feminine attraction.

The name was later given to the portable emergency radio on US navy life-rafts.

Gideon of Democracy, the: see *the Boss*.

Gipper, the: Ronald Reagan (b.1911), film actor and 40th US President. A reference to the part of George Gipp he played in the 1940 film *Knute Rockne — All-American*. Gipp had been a real life football star who died young. At one point, the surviving members of the team are exhorted to 'Win this one for the Gipper'.

In his autobiography, Reagan notes: 'Ever since my birth my nickname has been **Dutch** . . . my father claimed afterward that he was white when he said shakily, "For such a little bit of a fat Dutchman, he makes a hell of a lot of noise, doesn't he?"'

Later, for his matchless skills in addressing the American people on TV and radio — even when he may not have understood what he was talking about — he was dubbed **the Great Communicator.** For his skill in getting out of scrapes: **the Great Rondini.**

See also 'PRIVATE EYE' NICKNAMES.

Girl in the Red Velvet Swing, the: Evelyn Nesbit (*c.*1885–1967), American dancer and former Gibson Girl, who married the industrialist Harry K. Thaw. In 1906 Thaw shot Stanford White for what the newspapers called 'his exotic housekeeping' with the 22-year-old woman.

Give 'Em Hell Harry: Harry S Truman (1884–1972), 33rd President of the USA (1945–52). His campaign for re-election was mild until he told his running mate, Alben Barkly, 'I'm going to fight hard. I'm going to give them hell.' It caught on. Also known as **High Tax Harry** and **the Man from Missouri.**

Gladys: see 'PRIVATE EYE' NICKNAMES.

Gloriana: one of the many adulatory names for Elizabeth I, this one the invention of Edmund Spenser (*c.*1552–99) in his long allegoric poem *The Faerie Queene.* Another was similar — **Oriana,** or **the Peerless Oriana**, used in masques and madrigals, a cut above the humdrum **Good Queen Bess.** As to **the Virgin Queen,** how virginal she was is questionable, despite her never marrying or having children.

Glorious Iceberg, the: see *La Stupenda.*

Gnomes of Zurich: Swiss bankers and financiers. A term used to disparage the tight-fisted methods of the speculators in the Swiss financial capital who questioned Britain's creditworthiness and forced austerity measures on the Labour government of Prime Minister Harold Wilson when it came to power in 1964. The Secretary of State for Economic Affairs, George Brown, popularised the term. Harold Wilson had, however, first used it long before in a speech to the House of Commons on 12 November 1956, referring to 'all the little gnomes in Zurich and other finance centres'.

It became so embedded in the language that Swiss bankers would appear on television saying: 'Well, I am, how you say, a gnome?'

Goldenballs: see 'PRIVATE EYE' NICKNAMES.

Golden Boy: see POP STARS.

Golden Boy of British Football, the: see GOSSIP COLUMN NICKNAMES.

Golden Foghorn, the: see SHOW BUSINESS STARS.

Golden Girl of British Pop, the: see POP STARS.

Goldy: see *Noll*.

Goodtime George: see JAZZ MUSICIANS.

GOSSIP COLUMN NICKNAMES: Newspaper and magazine gossip columns when they are not dealing in tittle-tattle about the lives of people famous *for* something (and extending the interest to their spouses, lovers and offspring) are writing about people who have no real claim to attention except that they may be in fashionable society, have a lot of money, or behave curiously. Indeed, a feature of mid-twentieth century popular journalism has been the rise of people who seem to have little existence outside the gossip columns. A good nickname helps secure the reader's attention, however. The following selection is drawn from people who appeared with some regularity in British newspaper gossip columns of the 1960s, 70s and early 80s:

> **Adolf:** Jill Bennett, actress. Given to her by John Osborne, an ex-husband, for reasons one can only guess at.
> **Algy Cluff:** John Cluff, oil tycoon and one-time proprietor of the *Spectator*, was told by a school contemporary, Richard Boston, that he resembled the character 'Algernon Moncrieff' in a production of Wilde's *The*

Importance of Being Ernest. 'Algy' has become the name by which he is known.

Baron Bonkers: Dutch-born Baron Steven Bentinck, millionaire entrepreneur.

Bouncing Czech, the: Robert Maxwell, publisher. Inevitable, as he was born in Czechoslovakia. Also **Captain Bob.**

Bubbles: Lady Rothermere, society hostess and wife of a newspaper proprietor — formerly Rank starlet Beverley Brooks. She now bounces in an effervescent way but hates the nickname because she thinks it makes her sound frivolous. The very thought!

Cad, the: Peter Cadbury, entrepreneur with a reckless streak.

Count Dracula: (1) William Rees-Davies, Conservative MP, also known as **the One-Armed Bandit,** principally because he only has one arm. (2) Gunther Sachs, billionaire.

Dirty Dai: Dai Llewellyn, also known as **the Seducer of the Valleys.** It must have been something he used to get up to. Indeed his somewhat interesting sex life has been described by him in the press.

Dragon Lady: Lady Rendlesham, fashion editor turned shopkeeper.

Duchess, the: April Ashley, Britain's most celebrated sex-change person.

Five New Pence: David Shilling, hat designer. Inevitable after decimalisation.

Four-Letter Annie: Princess Anne — on account of her habit of barking at the press. She has been known on occasion to use the phrase 'Naff off'. Following some churlish behaviour on her part in 1982, the *Daily Mirror* replied with a front-page headline: 'NAFF OFF, ANNE'.

Fragrant Hackette, the: Lady Olga Maitland, gossip columnist and defence enthusiast.

Golden Boy of British Football, the: George Best — usually accompanied by the word 'former'.

Greek Pudding, the: Arianna Stassinopoulos, a writer.

Himself: Gerald Grosvenor, 6th Duke of Westminster, to his peasants (i.e. tenants and staff).

Hottie: Jane Birbeck, former girl-friend of James Hunt, the racing driver, who gave it to her. Short for 'hot loins'.

Ice-maiden, the: Angela Rippon, disciplined broadcaster, also known as **Head Girl.**

Iron Lady, the: Yoko Ono. See also sep. entry and 'PRIVATE EYE' NICKNAMES.

Kanga: Lady Tryon, Australian former 'adviser' to Prince Charles.

Keeks: Lady Carina Fitzalan-Howard, now wife of David Frost. She dislikes it heartily.

Little Gum Gum: John Selwyn Gummer (also **Bummer** or **Seldom Glummer**), Chairman of the Conservative Party (1983–). At Cambridge he was known as 'Little Gum Gum, son of Zorro'. A keen churchman and involved in publishing, he next acquired the nickname **Gas 'n' Gaiters.** On appointment as party chairman he was known to some as **Harpic** because he wished to sanitise parts of the party – or 'because he's going round the bend.'

Loins of Longleat, the: Lady Silvy Thynne, daughter of the Marquess of Bath. Does one hear an echo of the popular car-sticker 'We Have Seen the Lions of Longleat'?

Lord of the Pies: the Earl of Bradford, who has run several restaurants and sold pies.

Marg of Arg, the: Margaret, Duchess of Argyll, celebrated participant in the 'divorce of the century'.

Mark the Shark: Mark McCormack, agent for sports stars.

Melons: Lady Helen Windsor, for two very good reasons.

Mr & Mrs Mole: Andrew Lloyd-Webber, composer, and his first wife Sarah, when together. From a marked physical resemblance.

Mr Fix-It: Adnan Khashoggi, Saudi Arabian arms dealer.

Myrtle Poisson: Ragtrade name for Mr (Michael) Fish, menswear designer.

Naughty Nora: Lady (Nora) Docker (1906–83), former dancing girl who married Sir Bernard Docker, a wealthy motor tycoon in 1949. In the 1950s they became famous for the gusto with which they spent his money.

Nicaraguan Firecracker, the: Bianca Jagger, ex-wife of Mick Jagger. She was born there and tended to behave like one.

Occupational Hazard, the: Princess Anne's daughter

Zara, from a remark made by her mother: 'I am not particularly maternal — it's an occupational hazard of being a wife' (1981).

Oddjob: Roddy Llewellyn, former companion of Princess Margaret, now horticulturalist. Probably arose when he lived in a commune.

Our Val: Princess Michael of Kent. Said to have been bestowed by HM The Queen, no less, because of the German-born Princess's Valkyrie-like attributes. Also known as: **BTL** (for 'billiard table legs') and **Princess Tom** (from the name of her previous husband). During a broadcast in 1984, she confessed that her husband called her **Mrs Ogmore-Pritchard** because she was so tidy, as was the character in Dylan Thomas's *Under Milk Wood.*

Ping: Carl Alex Bismarck, party-goer (he has a brother Maximilian, nicknamed **Pong,** and a sister Gunilla, nicknamed **Bolla** — put the names together and what do you have?).

Pink Crimplene: Liz Brewer, party-organiser, who wears outrageous clothes.

Popeye: Lord Weidenfeld, publisher.

Pretty Thing: John Bentley, asset-stripper, from his good looks and, perhaps, the 1971 song 'Oh You Pretty Thing'.

Randy Andy: Prince Andrew. The alliteration was inevitable but he has appeared to support the suggestion by carrying on with various nubile bits of stuff. Also: **One Night Standrew.**

Shrimp, the: Jean Shrimpton, winsome-looking top model of the 1960s.

Snowdrop: the Earl of Snowdon. Also **Snowbum** and, at Buckingham Palace, **Snapshots.**

Sooty: Russell Harty, because of his teddy-bear appearance. The nickname had to be explained to him, too.

Spam: Lord Vestey, member of the family of butchers.

Teapot: The Marquess of Dufferin and Ava, because with those ears she looks like one?

Thunder-thighs: Tina Onassis, Greek shipping heiress. Believed to be a reference to their size rather than anything else.

Tiny: R. W. Rowland (born Roland Fuhrop), tycoon. Because he is tall. He signs his company reports 'Tiny Rowland'. Dubbed 'the unacceptable face of capitalism' by Edward Heath.

Whiplash Wallace: (or **Whipper**) Anna Hesketh, formerly Anna Wallace. One-time girl-friend of Prince Charles. Huntin'-mad.

(See also 'PRIVATE EYE' NICKNAMES − the names in these sections are largely interchangeable.)

Gov'nor, the: (1) Francis Albert (Frank) Sinatra (b.1915), American popular singer. In his twenties he was a teenage idol. His slight, boyish appearance gave him the first of several nicknames − **Bones.** Next, in the 1940s, he became known as **the Voice.** As he prospered − and perhaps because of alleged underworld connections − he became **the Chairman of the Board** or 'the Gov'nor'. After a temporary retirement, he returned, touting the rather commercially directed cry, **'Ol' Blue Eyes** is back.'
(2) George Edwardes. See SHOW BUSINESS STARS.
(3) Richard Blackwell. See *the Gaffer.*

Grandma Moses: Anna Mary Robertson Moses (1860−1961), American primitive artist.

Grandmother of Europe, the: see *the Widow at Windsor.*

Grand Old Man, the: (or GOM) (1) W.E.Gladstone, (1809− 98) four times Liberal Prime Minister. In 1882 the Earl of Iddesleigh said in a speech: 'Argue as you please, you are nowhere; that grand old man, the Prime Minister, insists on the other thing.' Also known as **the Great Commoner** because he refused a peerage. Critics interpreted GOM as **God's Only Mistake** or reversed the initials and said the **MOG** stood for 'the murderer of Gordon' (Gordon of Khartoum). From Gladstone's interest in reforming prostitutes, some of whom he took home to try to turn them from their way of life, came another name: **Old Glad Eye(s).** It was noted that he usually selected the pretty ones. He was familiar with some of the higher echelons of Victorian courtesans, including the notorious Skittles (Catherine Walters) whose salons he attended, along with the Prince of Wales, Lord Kitchener and aristocracy.

(2) W. G. Grace (1848—1915), cricketer, became known as **the Grand Old Man of English Cricket**. Also: **the Great Cricketer** and **the Champion**.

Grandpapa England: King George V (1865—1936), as known to his granddaughters, the Princesses Elizabeth and Margaret. However, in a 1983 biography of the Queen, Princess Margaret was reported as denying that she and her sister had ever used the nickname: 'We were much too frightened of him to call him anything but Grandpapa.'

Before he became heir apparent on the death of his brother Eddy, he was dubbed **Sprat** by his naval colleagues in contrast to the Prince of W(h)ales. Later he became **the Sailor Prince** and finally, like his ancestor William IV, **the Sailor King.** He never forgot his naval training — always punctilious about time and dress, always noting the state of the weather in his diary.

Grandpa's Grandson: Benjamin Harrison (1833—1901), 23rd US President (1889—93). His grandfather was William Henry Harrison, 9th President.

grass widow: originally a nickname for a woman living with a man to whom she is not married (sixteenth century), then as a divorced woman or discarded mistress. In recent times it has been modified to that of a wife whose husband has temporarily neglected her, being absent on business or for a sporting pursuit, the latter condition often being specified as 'golfing widow', 'angling widow' etc. (The analogy is a rural one, probably with a horse 'put out to grass', separated from others, resting.) With many wives now going out to work or enlarging their interests outside the home, a male counterpart of 'grass widower' has been introduced.

Great Beast, the: see *the Beast 666.*

Great Captain, the: see *the Iron Duke.*

Great Cham (of Literature), the: see *Dictionary Johnson.*

Great Commoner, the: (1) William Pitt the Elder (1708–78), three times first minister.

(2) W. E. Gladstone. See *the Grand Old Man*.

(3) Henry Clay. See *the Mill Boy of the Slashes*.

(4) William Jennings Bryan. See *the Boy Orator of the Platte*.

Great Communicator, the: see *the Gipper*.

Great Compromiser, the: see *the Mill Boy of the Slashes*.

Great Cricketer, the: see *the Grand Old Man*.

Great Emancipator, the: see *the Emancipator*.

Greatest Living Englishman, the: see 'PRIVATE EYE' NICKNAMES.

Great Magician, the: see *the Great Unknown*.

Great Moralist, the: see *Dictionary Johnson*.

Great Pacificator, the: see *the Mill Boy of the Slashes*.

Great Profile, the: see FILM STARS.

Great Rondini, the: see *the Gipper*.

Great Train Robbers, the: participants in the spectacular hold-up of a Glasgow-to-London train in Buckinghamshire, 1963, when £2,500,000 were stolen from the mail van. Newspaper headlines for the long-running story of arrests, trials, escapes and recaptures were inspired by the early silent film classic *The Great Train Robbery*, 1903. The robbers themselves had individual nicknames, e.g. Roy John James was **the Weasel,** Ronald Edwards was **Buster,** and Douglas Gordon Goody was **Checker.**

Great Unknown, the: Sir Walter Scott (1771–1832), in reference to the anonymous publication of his novels which, for ten years, were credited to 'the author of *Waverley*', the first of the series, 1814. He had gone into partnership with James Ballantyne, printer, and they hid the identity of authorship. Two eulogistic nicknames for him were **the Great Magician** and **Wizard of the North.**

great unwashed, the: working-class people, or the 'lower orders' in general, a term used by politician and writer Edmund Burke (1729–97), perhaps echoing Shakespeare's reference to 'Another lean unwash'd artificer' (*King John*, IV:ii).

Greek Pudding, the: see GOSSIP COLUMN NICKNAMES.

Green Goddess, the: Diana Moran, keep-fit demonstrator on BBC breakfast television from 1983. A well-preserved lady in her forties with blonde hair, she has worn distinctive green exercise clothing. Her nickname had previously been applied to a wartime fire engine, a Crème de Menthe cocktail, a lettuce salad, and a lily.

green ribbon men: seventeenth-century political opponents of the court, the early Whigs who met in taverns and coffee houses and wore a bow of green ribbon in their hats for identification. They were mainly associated with the King's Head tavern at the corner of Fleet Street and Chancery Lane, London, from about 1675, and here the news was discussed and plots hatched. It became an operational headquarters for the Whig faction, and many prominent men were members of the club. (Green was a colour of opposition from Cromwell's day.)

Greybacks: see *Bluejackets.*

Grim Grom: Andrei Andreyevich Gromyko (b.1909), Soviet foreign minister since 1957, so called by British officials because of his solemn expression.

Grocer, the: see 'PRIVATE EYE' NICKNAMES.

Grocer's Daughter, the: see *the Iron Lady.*

grog: rum diluted with water, as introduced by Admiral Edward Vernon (1684–1757), in an attempt to prevent scurvy among his crewmen, 1740 (it didn't). Vernon's nickname was **Old Grog** because of his addiction to a cloak made of grogram – a coarse material of silk and wool. The nickname was also given by sailors to public houses ashore – 'grog shop', a place where spirits were sold.

groundlings: spectators in the Elizabethan theatre who stood on the ground around the stage because they could not afford seats in the galleries. (A few privileged people sat on the stage itself.) Hence the extended meaning for the poorer section of the public. Public playhouses, circular or octagonal in shape (although the Fortune, built later, was square) had a stage in the middle of an open space with a roofed section at the back of it. The 'groundlings' crowded at the front and sides. In his instructions to the players who have come to the castle, Hamlet says: 'O! it offends me to the soul to hear a robustious periwig-pated fellow tear a passion to tatters, in very rage, to split the ears of the groundlings . . .' (*Hamlet*, III:ii). As theatre construction developed the cheaper seats were moved to the highest gallery in the house, and by early Victorian times it had become nicknamed 'the gods'.

Guinea Pigs, the: RAF pilots from the Second World War who suffered burns and were treated at the Queen Victoria Hospital, East Grinstead, under the noted plastic surgeon, Sir Archibald McIndoe. A Guinea Pig Club exists to take care of their welfare. It is headed by a Chief Guinea Pig. The name 'Guinea Pig' in this instance comes from the feeling that they were being experimented on to develop new techniques of surgery.

Guy the Gorilla: see CRICKETERS.

Gypsy Dave: see 'PRIVATE EYE' NICKNAMES.

H

hackettes: female journalists. The word is derived from the traditional name for any run-of-the-mill journalist, 'hack'. Principally a *Private Eye* usage.

ham: an actor with more enthusiasm than ability, one who would tend to 'tear a passion to tatters', as Hamlet put it in his instructions to the players (III:ii), hence the possible derivation. (And from which we get the expression, 'Hamming it up'.) Another explanation for the nickname is that theatrical make-up used to be removed with ham fat, and there was a song once popular in the USA about an actor called 'The Hamfat Man'. The nickname as applied to an amateur radio operator, coined in the 1920s, is more likely to refer to the amateur status.

Hammer, the: Sir David McNee (b.1925), Commissioner of the Metropolitan Police 1977–82. He was given the name by the *Scottish Daily Express* for his tough approach to law and order as a senior detective in Glasgow. It was revived when he moved to London. Clearly, derived from the following entry:

Hammer of the Scots, the: Edward I (1239–1307), although he was just as severe in his campaign against the Welsh; a great administrator as well as warrior. The plain slab under which he was buried in Westminster Abbey bore the inscription *Edwardus primus Scottorum malleus hic est*. Also called **Longshanks** because he was tall and good-looking.

Handsomest Man in the World, the: see FILM STARS.

Hanging Judge, the: John Toler (1745–1831), chief justice of the common pleas in Ireland, noted for his harsh treatment of rebels with whom he joked when passing sentence of death. He had a coarse sense of humour and a cruel streak, and according to *DNB* 'showed gross partiality, buffoonery, and scant legal knowledge on the bench'.

Happy: Mrs Nelson Rockefeller (b.1912), American society figure and widow of the Vice-President. According to a report in the *New York Times* (1983), a French nursemaid bounced baby Margaretta Fitler on her knee at the news that Charles Lindbergh had landed in France, 1927. The baby responded with a happy smile, leading the nursemaid to cry out, 'You are zee most happy baby I have ever seen.' That is how she acquired the name by which she is still known.

Harefoot: Harold I, illegitimate son of Canute whom he briefly succeeded as King of England in opposition to his legitimate brother, Hardicanute, whose mother — Queen Emma — was banished from the kingdom. He died in 1040. The nickname-surname by which he was known was probably given because of his speed in action; or there could have been a deformity.

Harpic: see GOSSIP COLUMN NICKNAMES.

Harvey Smith: a V-sign gesture given as a signal of disapproval. The show-jumping champion Harvey Smith gave it famously — and in view of the television audience — at Hickstead in 1971. It looked like contempt of Hickstead's owner, Douglas Bunn, but Smith argued that it was a 'Victory V'.

havelock: a cloth covering (usually white) for a soldier's cap, with a flap over the back of the neck as protection against sunstroke. Another eponymous nickname, commemorating Sir Henry Havelock (1795–1857) whose troops were the first to be issued with the headgear. It was this distinguished officer whose column relieved Lucknow in the Indian mutiny.

hawkubites: see *mochocks*.

Head Girl: see GOSSIP COLUMN NICKNAMES.

Hereward the Wake: heroic resistance fighter against the Norman conquerors of England, always watchful and alert against their incursions into his domain in the Lincolnshire fens. His exploits became legendary, and the nickname was awarded long after his death around the end of the eleventh century, as was another tribute, 'England's darling'. (Alfred 'the great' was also given the honorific, 'England's darling'.)

Hero of '77, the: see *the Fraud.*

Herr Schidt: see 'PRIVATE EYE' NICKNAMES.

Highland Laddie, the: see *the Young Pretender.*

High Tax Harry: see *Give 'Em Hell Harry.*

Hilda: see *the Iron Lady.*

Himself: see GOSSIP COLUMN NICKNAMES.

His Accidency: inevitable nickname for US Vice-Presidents, who succeed to the Presidency through death and have not been elected to the office. See *the Accidental President, the American Louis-Philippe, the Dude President, the Man of Destiny, Sir Veto.*

hobo: a migratory worker, nickname confined mainly to American speech but which has been raised to dictionary status; probably based on 'hoe-boy', although it may have some connection with the old English 'hob', a rustic. The name has been extended to mean a tramp.

Hockey Stick, the: see FILM STARS.

hocus pocus: Elizabethan nickname for a conjuror or fairground magician, bedazzling the crowds with mock-Latin incantations including these words. It was gradually extended to mean an imposter, or trickery and nonsense.

hodge: a yokel, simple countryman; probably derived from the servant in William Stevenson's play, *Gammer Gurton's Needle*, 1575.

Hollywood 10, the: see *Chicago 7.*

Holy Fool: see *Lord Porn.*

Holy Maid of Kent, the: see *the Nun of Kent.*

Honest Abe: see *the Emancipator.*

Honey Fitz: J. F. Fitzgerald (1863–1950), Mayor of Boston, Mass. and grandfather of President John F. Kennedy.

Hooray Henry: loud-mouthed 'upper class twit', chiefly interested in huntin', shootin' and fishin'. The archetypal Sloane Ranger husband is called Henry. He makes a meaningless noise, best rendered in print by putting 'hooray'. Originated in the jazz world *c.*1951.

hooverers: nickname invented for fishermen and their vessels using large nets to take up gigantic catches, then suctioning the contents in the manner of a vacuum cleaner, a technique that threatened European herring shoals in the 1970s.

hot gospeller: a fervent evangelist; old nickname for a Puritan preacher of hell-fire for sinners.

Hotspur: Henry Percy (1364–1403), eldest son of the 1st Earl of Northumberland, the nickname awarded when he was 20 because of his tireless and vigorous skirmishing along the Scottish border. From boyhood, Harry Hotspur was a fearless fighter and his valour in many battles became legendary; he was idolised by soldiers, esquires and knights — tall, handsome with black curling hair, but moody and with a hesitancy or thickness of speech. Shakespeare stresses his virtue and prowess in *I King Henry IV.*

Hotspur of Debate, the: see *the Rupert of Debate.*

Hottie: see GOSSIP COLUMN NICKNAMES.

Houdini in the White House: see *the Boss*.

Houdini of American Politics, the: see *Tricky Dick*.

Houdini of Politics, the: Harold Wilson, later Lord Wilson, (b.1916), Labour Prime Minister (1964–70, 74–76). Incidentally, he was known as 'Willie' at school. See also 'PRIVATE EYE' NICKNAMES.

Huguenots: French Protestants were given this nickname in the sixteenth century, and it grew into a title for them. One theory is that it was derived from the gate of King Hugo at Tours, near which followers of Luther used to meet at night. A monk ridiculed them in this way in a sermon. It may have coincided neatly with an old French word for a small pot. As with Quakers, a term of derision was honourably adopted and became familiar in England when many of them crossed the Channel to escape persecution from about 1685.

Hunchfront of Lime Grove, the: Sabrina (b.*c.*1938), busty model much remembered for her outstanding features displayed on TV shows with Arthur Askey in the 1950s. Real name: Norma Sykes. She later went to live in Hollywood. Perhaps not a widely used nickname, but a happy coinage of the time.

Hunt the Shunt: James Hunt (b.1947), world champion racing driver in 1976. So named in his early days because of a propensity for driving into things.

Hurricane Henry Armstrong: see BOXERS.

I

Ice-maiden, the: see GOSSIP COLUMN NICKNAMES.

Ike: Dwight D. Eisenhower (1890–1972), US general and 34th President (1953–61). The nickname 'Ike' was derived from his surname at school, although initially he was called 'Red Ike' (because of his hair) to distinguish him from the others. The name stuck throughout his military career and became even more popular as part of his winning slogan, 'I Like Ike'. ('Ike' is also late nineteenth-century American slang for an uncouth or stupid person'; 'Ikey' is a derogatory term for a Jew, from Isaac.)

Illinois Baboon, the: see *the Emancipator*.

Immortal Tinker, the: John Bunyan (1628–88) who worked at his father's trade as a tinker before becoming a soldier on the Parliamentary side and then turning to preaching and writing. It was probably during his second imprisonment that he began his famous work, *The Pilgrim's Progress*. Another honorific is 'the immortal dreamer'.

Iron Butterfly, the: see FILM STARS.

Iron Chancellor, the: Prince Otto E. L. Bismarck (1815–98), mainly responsible for making Prussia the most powerful of the German states. When the German Empire was formed in 1871 he became its first Chancellor. He declared his policy to be one of 'blood and iron'. He used these words in a speech to the Prussian parliament in 1862, and they seemed also to fit his own warlike and inflexible character.

Iron Duke, the: Arthur Wellesley, 1st Duke of Wellington (1769–1852), great soldier and statesman, as strong and unbending as Bismarck, but in his case the nickname was especially applicable when he erected iron shutters (and two cannons in the gateway) at his home, Apsley House, London, during riots in favour of the Reform Bill. It was appropriate, too, that large iron statues were set up in various parts of the country after his death.

Elizabeth Longford in her biography of Wellington (Weidenfeld & Nicolson, 1969–72) comments:

> *Punch* may be said to have coined the expression in 1845. Commenting on the regimental brevity of Wellington's epistolary style from which all 'small courtesies and minor graces' were omitted, *Punch* said: 'We cannot but think that Iron Dukes like Iron Pokers are none the worse for just a little polish.' If the term became popular only after the Duke's death, there were plenty of precedents earlier than 1845 for its subsequent adoption — from General Pakenham's admiration for 'the iron man', to his own frank pride in his 'iron hand'. His younger contemporary, the painter Frith, heard that after Waterloo he 'shed iron tears'.

He was also known as **Conkey** or **(Old) Nosey** because of his notable Roman nose and, after his victory at Waterloo, **the Great Captain.**

Iron Lady, the (of British Politics): Margaret Thatcher (b.1925), Conservative Prime Minister (1979–). On 19 January 1976 she said in a speech: 'The Russians are bent on world dominance . . . the Russians put guns before butter.' Within a few days, the Soviet Defence ministry newspaper *Red Star* had accused the 'Iron Lady' (sometimes translated as **Iron Maiden**) of seeking to revive the Cold War. The article wrongly suggested that she was known by this nickname in the UK at that time. A few days later Mrs Thatcher made the title her own in another speech. (The 'Iron Maiden of Nuremberg' was a medieval instrument of torture.)

Apart from this, Mrs Thatcher has proved singularly nick-name-prone:

Attila the Hen

Blessed Margaret, the: so called by Norman St John Stevas until he was removed from her Cabinet.

Boss, the: inevitably, but in fiction and in fact what her husband, Denis, calls her.

Cold War Witch, the: another Russian coinage.

Grocer's Daughter, the: indeed, she is one — but she also followed Edward Heath as Leader of the Conservative Party and he had been nicknamed *the Grocer*. See 'PRIVATE EYE' NICKNAMES.

Hilda: her middle name.

Leaderene, the

Milk Snatcher: when Education Secretary, she stopped the supply of free milk to school children. A rhyme of the time went: 'Thatcher, Thatcher, Milk Snatcher.'

Mrs Finchley: this arose from a slip of the tongue by David Dimbleby, presenting BBC TV's General Election coverage in 1983. Finchley is her suburban North London constituency.

Mother

Pasionaria of Privilege, La

Reluctant Debutante, the

She-Who-Must-Be-Obeyed: after the all-powerful Arabic queen, Ayesha, in H. Rider Haggard's novel *She* (1887).

Snobby Roberts: from her maiden name.

Tina: an acronym for 'There Is No Alternative' — an indication of her response when the Government's cuts in public spending were opposed in the summer of 1979.

Witch of Finchley, the

See also GOSSIP COLUMN NICKNAMES.

Ironside: Edmund (or Eadmund), son of Ethelred 'the Unready', because he was a valiant fighter and noted for his great strength. Edmund (*c*.980–1016), King of the West Saxons, fought against the Danes until a division of the kingdom was agreed upon, Canute ruling the north, Edmund the south.

Ironsides: Oliver Cromwell's cavalry at the start of the Civil War, the nickname bestowed on them, with respect, by Prince Rupert (who commanded his own horsemen on the royalist side) and who admired their discipline as well as their light armour. Rupert also called Cromwell himself 'Old Ironsides'.

Italian Alp, the: see BOXERS.

It Girl, the: Clara Bow (1905–65), popular actress of the silent film era who appeared in *It* (1928), based on an Elinor Glyn story, and other films of flapperdom. 'It' was the word used in billings to describe her vivacious sex appeal. Previously, 'it' had had more basic sexual connotations — such as survive in the expression 'to have it off'.

J

Jack: one of the most obliging nicknames in the language, with a multiplicity of uses, the diminutive of John or James (Jacobus). It was so familiar a name that it was used for the ordinary working man, 'every man jack' and 'jack of all trades'. We meet him in Jack Frost (personification of winter), Jack-a-Lent (a figure to throw balls and stones at in Lenten games), Jack-in-the-Green (usually a chimney sweep covered with leaves on May Day); and he pops up in jack-in-the-box, and rises above his station when he becomes a jack-in-office. As befitted his lowly status, Jack was also something small, like jacksprat (a dwarf), and the name was given to the small target wood rolled out first in a game of bowls; and he could be used in the nickname for an impudent fellow or coxcomb, coupled with that of a cheeky monkey, jackanapes − 'I will teach a scurvy jack-a-nape priest to meddle or make', says Caius in *The Merry Wives of Windsor*, I:iv. Jack is also a small flag on the jack-staff at the bow of a ship, indicating nationality, or Union Jack, bringing us back to King James, or Jacobus.

A 'jack' in medieval times was a waxed leather tankard, and also the quilted leather coat, often plated with metal, worn by the ordinary foot soldier, the latter having its own diminutive of our present-day jacket.

Jack Tar: a sailor, from the late eighteenth century, because his hat, jacket and breeches were made of cloth which was water-proofed with tar; the nickname often abbreviated to 'Tar'. (He was familiar enough with this commodity because much of his time was spent caulking the seams of ships with it, mixed with oakum.)

Jack the Ripper: the unknown murderer of several prostitutes in the East End of London (he was probably responsible for the deaths of eight), 1887—9, their mutilated bodies suggesting that he might have been a sex-maniac butcher, which was one of the theories about his identity; another was that the crimes were committed by a sailor, and another that they involved a member of the royal family. The murders were such a long-lasting sensation, that the nickname 'Ripper' was bestowed on subsequent perpetrators of similar crimes.

Jackal, the: Carlos Martinez (b.1949), Venezuelan-born assassin, who has worked with various terrorist gangs in several countries. A journalistic tag derived from the would-be assassin of Charles de Gaulle in Frederick Forsyth's novel *The Day of the Jackal*.

Jacobites: supporters of the House of Stuart for succession to the British throne in the persons of James II and his descendants; responsible for the risings of 1715 and 1745.

jakes: a very old and long persisting (although in recent times reduced to slang) nickname for lavatory, probably originating in the Elizabethan court when Sir John Harrington (1561—1612) invented a flush contraption for Hampton Court. Sir John was more closely commemorated by 'Jake's place' for WC.

James the White: the Duke of Ormonde in the Irish peerage (1610—88) who commanded the Royalists against the Parliamentary army when Cromwell rampaged in Ireland. Portraits show that he had long fair hair, sweeping below the shoulders, and it was probably lighter than it looks. He was Lord Lieutenant of Ireland and was Lord High Steward at the coronations of Charles II and James II.

Jaybotham: see 'PRIVATE EYE' NICKNAMES.

JAZZ MUSICIANS: Whereas gangsters have tended to incorporate nicknames in the middle of their names, jazz musicians have more often — though not invariably — substituted nicknames for their first names: hence Edward Kennedy Ellington is invariably known as 'Duke' Ellington (see *Duke*). A small selection:

Charles (Charlie) **Bird** Parker (1920—55), alto saxist — also **Yardbird**.

William **Count** Basie (1904—84), band leader. A Kansas City radio interviewer in 1926, commenting on 'the royal family of jazz', said there was the King of Oliver and the Duke of Ellington, 'How about the Count of Basie?' Towards the end of his life, however, Basie admitted: 'I hated the name Count. I wanted to be called Buck or Hoot or even Arkansas Fats.'

John Birks **Dizzy** Gillespie (b.1917), trumpeter.

Jean Baptiste **Django** Reinhardt (1910—53), guitarist.

Earl **Fatha** Hines (1905—83), influential American pianist.

Fats: Thomas Waller (1904—43), American pianist, always known as Fats Waller.

Goodtime George: George Melly (b.1926), critic and jazz singer, celebrated in a song with this title, written by John Chilton.

Jelly Roll: Ferdinand Joseph Le Menthe Morton (1885—1941), pianist and one of the creators of New Orleans jazz. 'Jelly-roll' is slang for the female vagina, for a virile man, or for sundry other sexually connected activities. It occurred among Negroes in the South and became incorporated in the lyrics of early jazz songs, not least Morton's.

Edward **Kid** Ory (1886—1973), trombonist and vocalist.

Joe **King** Oliver (1885—1938), cornetist and composer.

King of Swing, the: Benny Goodman (b.1909), clarinettist and band leader.

Lady Day: Billie Holiday (1915—59), singer.

Leadbelly: Huddie Leadbetter (1889—1949), blues singer — a corruption of his name and a reference to his strength — he had a buckshot wound in his stomach.

Muddy Waters (b.1915), blues singer (real name: McKinley Morganfield). So nicknamed by his grandmother because he frequently played in Deer Creek as a child.

Francis Joseph **Muggsy** Spanier (1906—67), cornetist.

Charles Ellsworth **Pee-Wee** Russell (1906—69), clarinettist and saxist.

Prez: Lester Young (1909—59), tenor saxophonist. He was

given the nickname by Billie Holiday. It stood for 'the President'.

John Haley **Zoot** Sims (b.1925), player of the clarinet, the tenor and alto saxophone.

See also *Satchmo*.

Jelly Roll: see JAZZ MUSICIANS.

Jemmy Twitcher: John Montagu, 4th Earl of Sandwich (1718–92), an extremely unpopular man, partly because of widespread corruption in the navy when he was First Lord of the Admiralty, partly because he turned against his friend John Wilkes, and took a leading part in prosecuting him, the latter behaviour earning him the nickname from the *Beggar's Opera*. A publication, the *Life, Adventures, Intrigues and Amours of the celebrated Jemmy Twitcher*, 1770 was libellous. Sandwich was a hell-fire rake in his youth. Nevertheless, his name has gone into history because Captain Cook named the Sandwich Islands after him, and he is remembered for a way of eating meat between two slices of bread.

Jersey Joe: see BOXERS.

Jersey Lily, the: Lily Langtry (1852–1929), beautiful actress, born in Jersey, daughter of a dean, who made her London debut in *She Stoops to Conquer*, 1881. She became an intimate friend of Edward VII when Prince of Wales.

Jewel of the Ghetto, the: see BOXERS.

Jewish American Princess: (usually **JAP**) this is the nickname for a type of upwardly mobile woman who wants to be rich and well married and believes that there is a formula for achieving this. She is notable, therefore, for wearing the right clothes, for her lacquered hair and carefully tended fingernails, and for her jewellery. Perhaps she would like to emulate that non-JAP, Jackie Kennedy Onassis — indeed, she does not have to be Jewish or American. The type occurs in most societies. There is a male equivalent.

Jezebel: a shamelessly flirtatious and probably immoral woman, especially one who uses make-up to lure men, as did Jezebel whom Ahab married, and who 'When Jehu came to Jezreel . . . she painted her eyes, and adorned her head, and looked out of the window' (2 *Kings*, 19). A mock letter in *The Spectator*, No. 175, 1711, is from a studious bachelor who complains of the distraction of the woman across the street: 'You are to know, Sir, that a Jezebel (so called by the neighbourhood from displaying her pernicious charms at her window) appears constantly dressed at her sash, and has a thousand little tricks and fooleries to attract the eyes of all the idle young fellows.'

Jiminy Peanuts/ Jimmy Who? see *President Peanut*.

Jix: William Joynson-Hicks, 1st Viscount Brentford (1865–1932), British politician who held several high offices, including those of Postmaster-General, Financial Secretary to the Treasury, Minister of Health and Home Secretary. He was also concerned with air and military affairs.

Jockey of Norfolk, the: John Howard, 1st Duke of Norfolk (*c.*1430–85), distinguished soldier on the Yorkist side and in France, created Duke and Earl Marshal by Richard III to whose allegiance he had turned. He was killed at Bosworth. He is referred to by this nickname in *King Richard III* (V:iii) when a mocking verse is sent to him on the battlefield, beginning, 'Jockey of Norfolk be not too bold . . . ' Like his descendants he may have been fond of horse-racing, but the word 'jockey' was also a form of Jacky, the diminutive of Jack and John, and it was also a convenient name for his enemies to use because 'jockey' in addition stood for cheat, due to the bad reputation of horse-traders.

According to the Creevey papers, the 11th Duke was also so nicknamed.

Joe Miller: at first a joke, then a worn-out joke — a 'chestnut' from long usage; named after Joe Miller (1684–1738), a popular comedian.

Joey: a handicapped person or someone behaving like one.

The children's TV programme *Blue Peter* featured a quadra-plegic spastic called Joey Deacon who was unable to com-municate in normal language. The idea was to promote a caring attitude in young viewers. Alas, cruelly, the word 'Joey' came to be used by children in quite the wrong way, as in 'You are a Joey', or 'That was a real Joey thing to do'. (The word is also applied, incidentally, to owls, to clowns — backstage, in honour of Grimaldi's Joey the Clown — and to a hunchback's hunch, among other things.)

John Bull: nickname — personification of the Englishman and his character, the origin is obscure but probably inspired by the organist and composer John Bull (1563–1628) who is believed to have composed the first national anthem. The name was not popularised until early in the eighteenth century, mainly through the anti-French writings of John Arbuthnot. Cartoonists built up an image of a stolid, fearless (sometimes boorish) country gentleman in riding jacket and top boots, and pamphleteers credited him with rugged common sense, patriotism and affability.

John Doe: legal invention from the nineteenth century (a fictitious name for a plaintiff when preparing or arguing a case, usually in ejectment actions) which became a nick-name for the man-in-the-street. The hypothetical defendant was called Richard Roe, but this name remained as legal jargon, as did another, John Noakes.

Jolly Jack: J. B. Priestley (1894–1984), prolific Yorkshire actor and playwright. An ironic nickname, as he was a champion grumbler.

K

K: Kenneth Clark (1903–83) (later Lord Clark), art historian, always so called by his chums. See also 'PRIVATE EYE' NICKNAMES.

Kaffir King, the: Barnett (Barney) Isaacs Barnato (1852–97), Anglo-Jewish financier and speculator in the Kimberley diamond industry and in South African gold mines. His financial ramifications were known as 'the kaffir circus'. Heavy losses ensued. He jumped from a ship sailing from Cape Town and was drowned.

Kaiser Bill: (1) Kaiser Wilhelm II (1859–1941), German Emperor and King of Prussia (1888–1918). A jocular way of dealing with the enemy during the First World War. Cartoonists used the nickname especially, depicting the Kaiser with an arrogant W-shaped moustache and spiked helmet.
(2) William Davis. See 'PRIVATE EYE' NICKNAMES.

Kanga: see GOSSIP COLUMN NICKNAMES.

Keeks: see GOSSIP COLUMN NICKNAMES.

Keith: see 'PRIVATE EYE' NICKNAMES.

Ken Leninspart: see 'PRIVATE EYE' NICKNAMES.

kevanhuller: eponymous nickname for a laced or braided hat, the brim pinched-in at one side, reminding us of Ludwig Andreas Kevenhuller (1683–1744) – the name variously spelt – Austrian Field Marshal who set the fashion. His successes against the French and Bavarians were publicised in England. Commenting on the oddities of fashion, *The Connoisseur* of 1754 (No. 36) remarked: ' . . . but we must, indeed, allow it to be highly ornamental, as the present hats worn by the women are more bold and impudent than the broad brimmed staring Kevanhullers worn a few years ago by the men.'

Kid, the: see FILM STARS.

Kid Ory: see JAZZ MUSICIANS.

Kim: H. A. R. Philby (b.1912), journalist and Soviet agent working as the head of anti-Soviet operations in the British intelligence service until he finally defected to Moscow in 1963. He was nicknamed 'Kim' at an early age, after the hero of Kipling's novel. He was born in the Punjab.

King, the: see *Elvis the Pelvis*.

King Andrew: see *Old Hickory*.

King Arthur: Arthur Scargill (b.1938), elected President of the National Union of Mineworkers, 1983 — a dominating, self-assured Yorkshireman. This journalistic tag when reporting his many government-defying activities and pronouncements not only evokes the actual King but also 'King Coal', the nineteenth-century term for a principal ingredient of the Industrial Revolution.

King Bomba: Ferdinand II, King of the Two Sicilies (1810—59). So named for his bombardment of Messina.

King Dick: see *Queen Dick*.

King Jog: J. G. Lambton, 1st Earl of Durham (1792—1840), because he said: 'One can jog along on £40,000 a year.'

Kingledon: the Wimbledon lawn tennis courts, named thus by the *Daily Mirror* in 1972 in honour of the American player Billie Jean King when she won the singles championship for the fourth time. She took the title for the sixth time in 1975 and announced that it might be her last appearance — but it wasn't. She was also one of the greatest doubles players.

King-Maker, the: Richard Neville, Earl of Warwick (1428–71), valiant fighter on the Yorkist side against the Lancastrians, secured the throne for his cousin, Edward of York, but because of the king's intrigues Warwick turned against him and for a short period ruled England himself as lieutenant of Henry VI whom he released from prison. Edward defeated his army and Warwick was killed at Barnet. Lord Lytton's novel, *The Last of the Barons*, tells his story.

King of Bath, the: see *Beau Nash*.

King of Calypso, the: see POP STARS.

King of Glam Rock, the: see POP STARS.

King of Hollywood, the: see FILM STARS.

King of Rock 'n' Roll, the: see *Elvis the Pelvis*.

King of Swing, the: see JAZZ MUSICIANS.

King of the Cowboys, the: see FILM STARS.

King of the Serials, the: see FILM STARS.

King Oliver: (1) Oliver Cromwell. See *Nosey*. (2) See JAZZ MUSICIANS.

knights of the road: see *gentlemen of the road*.

L

Lackland: King John (1167–1216), fourth and youngest son of Henry II and Eleanor of Aquitaine (who was 44 when she gave birth), because, unlike his brothers, he was given no feudal possessions in England or France. He was also known as John Lackland throughout his youth, and the French nicknamed him 'dollheart' when he fled from the siege of Roche-aux-Moines in 1214, although he had stronger forces than Louis who was dubbed 'Louis the Lion' (in contradistinction with John's brother, Richard the Lionheart). John had an eventful and troublous reign, and he is remembered mainly for the great charter – Magna Carta – which his barons extracted from him in 1215, granting liberties and justice.

Lad 'Imself, the: see SHOW BUSINESS STARS.

Lady Bird Johnson: Mrs Lyndon B. Johnson (b.1912), widow of President Johnson. 'Why she's as pretty as a lady bird!' nurse Alice Tittle described her charge, Claudia Alta Taylor, when the youngster was 2 years old. So she became known as Lady Bird Taylor. She happened to marry a man whose first names were Lyndon Baines, thus enabling her to continue enjoying the initials LB. Their daughters were christened Linda Baines and Lucy Baines. After the ex-President's death, her bank account continued to be in the name of Mrs L. B. Johnson and she still signs her correspondence (1983) as Lady Bird Johnson. She 'finds her name to be embarrassing only "overseas in the company of royalty" when those introduced to her for the first time are apt to ask in astonishment, "Lady Who?"'

lady bountiful: a generous benefactress in her locality, based on the character of the squire's mother in Farquhar's comedy *Beaux Stratagem*, 1707.

Lady Day: see JAZZ MUSICIANS.

Lady Forkbender: see 'PRIVATE EYE' NICKNAMES.

Lady Magnesia Freelove: see 'PRIVATE EYE' NICKNAMES.

Lady of Christ's, the: see *the Blind Poet.*

lady of pleasure: one of many euphemistic nicknames for a prostitute.

Lady with the Lamp, the: Florence Nightingale (1820–1910), philanthropist and nursing pioneer, in commemoration of her services to soldiers at Scutari during the Crimean War (1853–6). By dogged determination, skill and administrative ability she reformed the slipshod and insanitary conditions in the treatment of wounded soldiers, and she inspected hospital wards at night, carrying her lamp – a Turkish lantern consisting of a candle inside a collapsible shade. The phrase was coined by Longfellow in his poem *Santa Filomena* (1858):

> Lo! in that hour of misery
> A lady with a lamp I see
>   Pass through the glimmering gloom,
>   And flit from room to room.
> And slow, as in a dream of bliss
> The speechless sufferer turns to kiss
>   Her shadow, as it falls
>   Upon the darkening walls.

Florence Nightingale made nursing, hitherto a lowly occupation, respectable.

Lake Poets, the: Wordsworth, Coleridge and Southey who lived in, or visited, the Lake District in north-west England and were inspired by its scenery; sometimes called the 'Cumberland poets', although the Lake District spreads over Westmorland and north Lancashire as well. Critics used the nickname 'Lake school' in a rather derisory manner.

lame duck: someone handicapped by misfortune or by his own incapacity; a defaulter on the Stock Exchange by mismanagement or bad luck. It was a stigma to be shunned in the nineteenth century, but became softened in the twentieth. The money-conscious old Mr Osborne in Thackeray's *Vanity Fair* was suspicious of the financial position of Amelia's father: 'I'll have no lame duck's daughter in my family' (ch. xiii).

In the USA, the term came to be applied to a President or other office-holder whose power is diminished because he is about to leave office. In *c*.1970, it was also applied to British industries unable to survive without government support.

Larry: Laurence Olivier (Lord Olivier) (b.1907), the most famous English actor of the twentieth century. His nickname 'Larry', though obviously a diminutive of Laurence, has become so well known — in its stylish, actorish way — well beyond the bounds of his profession, that it merits inclusion here.

Last Chance Trendy or **LCT:** a man on the brink of middle age who dresses younger than he should, carefully sculpts his hair over incipient baldness, and behaves as if youth is going out of style.

Last Man, the: Charles I (1600–49), as the Parliamentarians called him, wishfully thinking he would be the last of royalty in England. Royalists rejoindered with **Son of the Last Man** for Charles II. Defeated in the Civil War by Parliamentary forces he was convicted of treason and beheaded at Whitehall, London, meeting his death with great dignity — **the Royal Martyr.**

Last of the Cocked Hats, the: James Monroe (1758–1831), 5th President of the USA (1817–25). So called as a notable survivor of the third quarter of the eighteenth century when cocked hats were in vogue (and when the Declaration of Independence was signed).

Last of the Red Hot Mommas, the: see SHOW BUSINESS STARS.

Last of the Saxons, the: King Harold (*c.*1026—66) who has perhaps a better claim than Hereward to be 'Last of the English', son of Earl Godwin; killed at the Battle of Hastings when William of Normandy ('the Conqueror') invaded to claim the throne.

LCT: see *Last Chance Trendy.*

Leadbelly: see JAZZ MUSICIANS.

Leaderene, the: see *the Iron Lady.*

Leather Lungs: see POP STARS.

Levellers: political group, mainly of soldiers in the Parliamentary army during the Civil War, advocating reforms under the leadership of John Lilburne.

Li'l Arthur: see BOXERS.

Lillian Russell: see *mae west.*

Lillibet: Queen Elizabeth II (b.1926) — a childhood mispronunciation of her name by sister Margaret which was taken up by the rest of the family. See also 'PRIVATE EYE' NICKNAMES.

limey: (short for 'lime-juicer'), near-slang for a British sailor in the eyes of his Australian and American counterparts, from the practice (since the early nineteenth century) of issuing lime juice to prevent scurvy; extended to include any Briton.

Lion of Judah, the: Haile Selassie, Emperor of Ethiopia (Abyssinia) from 1930 until his dethronement in 1974, with the exception of the Italian occupation, 1936—41. He was a founder of the Organisation of African Unity.

Lion of the North, the: Gustavus Adolphus or Gustavus II (1594—1632), King of Sweden. A brilliant general, he waged successful wars with Denmark, Poland and Russia and fought in the Thirty Years' War. He was killed at the Battle of Lutzen.

Little Aussie Bleeder, the: see SHOW BUSINESS STARS.

Little Black Banda: Dr Hastings Banda (b.1906), President of Malawi since 1966. Early 1960s coinage, echoing 'Little Black Sambo' of the children's tale.

Little Corporal, the: see *Boney*.

Little Egypt: see SHOW BUSINESS STARS.

little Englander: one who regards England as sufficient in itself, or indicating a narrowness of outlook on the international scene; applied originally to the opponents of imperialism and colonisation in Victorian times.

Little Flower, the: Fiorello La Guardia (1882—1947), conspicuous Mayor of New York. A translation of his first name.

Little Giant, the: Stephen A. Douglas (1813—61), US Democratic statesman. In 1858, the 'Little Giant' stood against Abraham Lincoln — and defeated him — in the Illinois senatorial campaign, though the nickname may date from an earlier triumph. In 1834 he defeated President Andrew Jackson's attack on the National Bank in a debate with Josiah Lambon.

Little Gum Gum: see GOSSIP COLUMN NICKNAMES.

Little Magician: Martin van Buren (1782—1862), 8th President of the USA (1837—41). Also known as the **Wizard of Kinderhook** or **Old Kinderhook** (from the farm where he was born in the State of New York).

Little Miss Dynamite: see POP STARS.

Little Mo: Maureen Connolly, American tennis star and a Wimbledon favourite. She won the championship there three times, 1952–54. She won her first championship at Forest Hills in 1951 when only sixteen. Her tennis career ended after an accident in 1954.

Little Sparrow, the: Edith Piaf (1915–63), small French singer. Her real name was Edith Gassion. 'Piaf' is French slang for sparrow or little sparrow.

Little Sure-Shot: Annie Oakley (1860–1926), a remarkably skilful rifle-shooter from childhood. When she joined Buffalo Bill's Wild West Show, touring the USA and Europe, her marksmanship became legendary. On a visit to England in 1887 she performed before Queen Victoria. One of her tricks was to shoot a hole in a playing card thrown into the air, or to pierce each 'pip' in a card used as a target; hence an American nickname for a punched ticket, an 'Annie Oakley'. The musical play *Annie Get Your Gun* was based on her story.

Little Tich: Harry Relph (1868–1928), a popular music hall comedian performed under this name. Probably invented by his family when he was a baby, the nickname derived from the sensational Tichborne case – about the claim made in 1866 by a man from Australia that he was the missing heir to a Hampshire baronetcy and fortune. The Tichborne Claimant (Arthur Orton), who was imprisoned for perjury, was plump – as no doubt was Harry Relph as a little boy. Relph remained small in stature and, at first, called himself 'Little Tichbourne'. **Tich** then became the nickname for anyone small.

Little Waster, the: see SHOW BUSINESS STARS.

Little Willie: (1) Friedrich Wilhelm, Crown Prince of Germany, eldest son of the Kaiser of the First World War, so named by British troops. He commanded an army group, followed his father into exile in Holland, and renounced his rights of succession, 1918.

(2) A little boy's penis — 'Will' being a nickname for the male organ from the sixteenth century and used as such by Shakespeare in his sonnets, according to some interpreters.

Liver Lips: see POP STARS.

Livermore Larruper, the: see BOXERS.

Living Legend, the: see DISC JOCKEYS.

Lobsters: see *redcoats*.

Log Cabin Candidate, the: see *Tippecanoe*.

Loins of Longleat, the: see GOSSIP COLUMN NICKNAMES.

Lollards: a fourteenth-century nickname for followers of John Wycliffe, but used earlier in Holland for a group of Franciscans who questioned the authority of the Pope, hence a possible explanation of the word — from old Dutch meaning to hum or to sing softly (cf. our own 'lull' or 'lullaby') or from a word meaning an idler (cf. 'loll'). In the seventeenth century the Independents often expressed appreciation of a sermon by humming. But a strong contender to the derivation is *lolium*, tare, a poisonous weed. Chaucer must have had this source in mind when the shipman in *The Canterbury Tales* speaks of 'This Loller heer wil prechen us somwhat. . . Or springen cokkel in our clene corn.' Lollards aroused much enmity during Wycliffe's lifetime and after. Gower in his *Confessio Amantis*, 1393, referred to:

> This newe secte of lollardie
> And also many an heresie.

And John Audley early in the fifteenth century wrote: 'Lef thou me, a Loller, his deeds they will him deem. . . Never for him pray.' (Take it from me, a Lollard is known by his deeds. . .)

lollipop lady (or **man**): warden of a pedestrian crossing with special responsibilities for children, carrying a pole with a red warning disc on top which could be likened to the lollipop sweet of juvenile delight.

Lollo, La: see FILM STARS.

Long Cecil: a gun made by Cecil Rhodes's mining engineers as part of the defence of Kimberley in the Boer War, between October 1899 and February 1900.

Longshanks: see *the Hammer of the Scots*.

Long Tom: see *the Sage of Monticello*.

Lord Clark of Civilisation: see 'PRIVATE EYE' NICKNAMES.

Lord Fanny: Alexander Pope's unkind nickname for a clever but probably 'affected' man — John Hervey, Baron Hervey of Ickworth (1696—1743), Vice-Chamberlain to George II and Lord Privy Seal, statesman and able writer who made some powerful enemies. He was involved in intrigue, and — although physically weak and suffering from epilepsy — he fought a duel. He maintained a rigid diet, which his opponents ridiculed, and was said to use cosmetics, hence Pope's other nicknames of Adonis and Narcissus. Pope may have been jealous of his friendship with Lady Mary Wortley Montagu.

Lord Gnome: see 'PRIVATE EYE' NICKNAMES.

Lord Haw-Haw: William Joyce (1906—46) who broadcast Nazi propaganda from Hamburg during the Second World War, speaking in a cultured voice which the *Daily Express* radio correspondent Jonah Barrington ridiculed with this nickname. It was widely adopted and became a valuable antidote to the subversive announcements of German victories which Joyce put out, his supposed information about the success of bombing attacks on Britain, and his threats. He was found guilty of treason after the war and hanged.

Lord Look-on: Lord Lucan, a military commander whose troops in the Crimean War considered he didn't spend enough time in actual combat, especially when he missed a chance to charge a body of Russian cavalry in 1854.

Lord of the Pies: see GOSSIP COLUMN NICKNAMES.

Lord Porn: a British press nickname for Frank Pakenham (b.1905), 7th Earl of Longford, during a vigorous campaign he waged against pornography and sexual licence generally in the 1970s. A Labour Party representative in the House of Lords, he acquired a reputation for reforming zeal based on religious conviction. In 1972 he headed an unofficial group to inquire into pornography and the decline of moral standards. He urged higher penalties for pornographic offences, a new definition of the law of obscenity, a clean-up of books, films and television programmes, and the banning of sex education in schools without parental consent. A great publicist for his causes he does not appear to object to another nickname, **the Holy Fool.**

Lord Whelks: see 'PRIVATE EYE' NICKNAMES.

Lothario: (or **Gay Lothario**) a philanderer, seducer or rake, from a character in an early eighteenth-century play, *The Fair Penitent.*

lotus-eaters: those who live in luxury, standing aside from life and usually living abroad, hedonists in dreamful ease; an extension from the ancient Greek belief in a Libyan tribe that ate a fruit which produced a happy forgetfulness, a pleasurable idleness. Homer tells of Odysseus reaching such a country where many of his sailors ate the lotus and lost all desire to return home.

Louisville Lip, the: see BOXERS.

Lovell the Dog: Francis, Viscount Lovell (1454–87), Lord Chamberlain to Richard III and a loyal supporter, so that he was derided as the king's spaniel. His enemies circulated a rhymed couplet around London:

> The catte, the ratte and Lovell our dogge,
> Rulyth all England under a hogge.

The 'rat' was Sir Richard Ratcliffe, the 'cat' Sir William Catesby, speaker of the House of Commons, and the 'hog' was the King himself because he had a white boar on his coat-of-arms.

Love Rouser, the: see BOXERS.

Lucky: (1) 7th Earl of Lucan (b.1934) who disappeared in 1974 after being suspected of murdering his children's nanny.

(2) Salvatore Luciana, Sicilian−American racketeer (1896−1962), known as Lucky Luciano after he survived having his throat slit by a rival gangster.

See also BOXERS.

Luddites: a nickname revived in the late 1970s and early 80s for trade unionists who try to hamper technical progress − through microtechnology, for example − because of the threat to their jobs. The name was originally given to workers more violent in their protests in the early years of the Industrial Revolution when mechanisation caused unemployment and distress in the Midlands and northern counties of England. Textile workers carried out machine-wrecking raids, and there were serious riots between 1811 and 1816, the secret ringleaders going under the name of Captain (or King) Ludd. It is believed that the name was adopted accidentally from that of a Leicestershire boy − Ned Ludd − who was caught up in the trouble.

M

macaronis: late eighteenth-century dandies, men-about-town, usually addicted to gambling, drinking and duelling. They formed a Macaroni Club in London about 1760, the original members being young men who had made the tour to Italy and professed a liking for that country's speciality of wheaten flour moulded into tubes. The word persisted into the next century as a nickname for elegant fops, and was even in use in Edwardian times.

Machiavelli of Massachusetts, the: see *the Colossus of (American) Independence*.

Mac the Knife: (1) Harold Macmillan. See *Supermac*.

(2) Ian McIntyre (b.1931) who, when Controller of BBC Radio 4, instituted programme changes which created a mild furore, 1977–8.

(3) Ian MacGregor (b.1912), American–Scottish Chairman of the British Steel Corporation and then the National Coal Board in the 1980s, when making work-force redundant.

These — perhaps inevitable — applications all stem from the Brecht/Weill villain of *The Threepenny Opera*, based on MacHeath in *The Beggars' Opera*.

Mac the Mouth: see *Superbrat*.

Macwonder: see *Supermac*.

Mad: is a standard adjunct to the names of (usually) reckless military figures, e.g. (1) **Mad Anthony Wayne:** (1745–96) so called for his reckless heroism in the American Revolutionary War. He mounted a surprise attack on the British garrison at Stony Point on the Hudson in 1779.

(2) **Mad Mitch:** Lt-Col Colin Mitchell (b.1925), mentioned

in dispatches from Aden (1967). Briefly a Conservative MP.

(3) **Mad Mike:** Mike Hoare, South African mercenary in the Congo in the 1960s with the 'Wild Geese' commandos. In 1981 he led an abortive coup against the Seychelles government.

(4) **Mad Jack:** Jack Howard, 20th Earl of Suffolk and Berkshire (d.1941). He died defusing a bomb and was posthumously awarded the George Cross. He used to shoot champagne corks off with his revolver.

Mad Monk, the: Grigori Efimovich (*c.*1871−1916), known as Rasputin. Of Siberian peasant origin, he was famous for his debauchery and the influence he exercised over Tsarina Alexandra. He was murdered by a group of Russian noblemen (cf. entry in 'PRIVATE EYE' NICKNAMES). *Rasputin the Mad Monk* was the title used in Britain for the 1932 Hollywood picture *Rasputin and the Empress.*

Mad Mullah, the: nickname shared by two Mohammedan leaders of revolt against British administration (and allies) − one the 'Mad Mullah of Swat' in the Indian risings of 1897−8, and the better-known Mohammed bin Abdullah who created terror for tribes friendly to the British in Somaliland from 1899 until 1920 when he fled to Ethiopia.

In the plural, the name was reapplied to Iranian religious leaders in the turmoil following the fall of the Shah (1979), especially the Ayatollah Khomeini.

Mad Poet, the: Nathaniel Lee (*c.*1653−92), dramatist as well as poet. He wrote plays in verse and a tragedy, *The Rival Queens,* which had some success. Hard drinking affected his brain and he was confined to Bedlam for a time.

mae west: inflatable life-jacket issued to the services in the Second World War, the nickname coined by the RAF in tribute to the curvaceous American film star, Mae West (1892−1980) and then adopted as the official description, with the full approval of the buxom lady. Said she: 'I've been in *Who's Who* and I know what's what but this is the first time I've ever been in a dictionary.' Mae West, gay and uninhibited, first came into prominence in the film *She Done Him Wrong,* 1933, based on her play, *Diamond Lil.* Her catchphrase, 'Come up and see me some time' was for long on people's lips.

(It is interesting to recall that an earlier American actress with a plump figure, Lillian Russell (1861–1922) gave her name to a fashion popular in England as well as in her own country. The **Lillian Russell** ensemble beatified the hourglass figure, with sweeping bosom and a gown with a train, the lady wearing a large Gainsborough hat bedecked with feathers or flowers.)

Magnificent Wildcat, the: see FILM STARS.

Maid of Orleans: better known as Joan of Arc (1412–31), heroine of history and legend, who was inspired to lead the French army in the defence of Orleans when it was besieged by English and Burgundian forces. She was eventually captured by the Burgundians who handed her over to the English, and they burned her at the stake in the market place at Rouen, condemned of witchcraft. Her canonisation as St Joan did not take place until 1920. The French call her **La Pucelle** ('maiden'). Recent research has questioned her peasant origin, and doubt has even been cast on whether it was she who was burned at the stake.

Manassa Mauler, the: see BOXERS.

Man from Missouri, the: see *Give 'Em Hell Harry*.

Man in Leather Breeches, the: George Fox (1624–91), founder of Quakerism. The nickname was bestowed on him in his early years as an itinerant preacher. As he walked or rode throughout Britain people would shout, 'The man in leather breeches is come!' according to his own account in his *Journal*. The reason is not clear, because leather breeches for riding were not uncommon. He probably made them himself: as a boy he was apprenticed to a shoemaker and worked in leather.

Man in the Iron Mask, the: mysterious prisoner in the reign of Louis XIV of France who was never seen without a mask (probably velvet on an iron frame). He died unidentified in the Bastille in 1703. Many conjectures about his identity have been made (including that of Alexandre Dumas in his novel of that name), some that he was an illegitimate member of the royal family.

Man-in-the-Street, the: the ordinary citizen whom politicians, sociologists and investigators of all kinds court, question and in theory revere. His (and her) opinions began seriously to be considered by Mass Observation in the 1930s, and this task has been extended by 'Opinion Polls', letters to newspapers, *vox pop* interviews for radio and television, and 'phone-ins' for broadcast programmes. He has been variously described as 'Tom, Dick and Harry' and 'grass roots'.

Man of a Thousand Faces, the: see FILM STARS.

Man of Destiny, the: (1) Napoleon Bonaparte. See *Boney*.
   (2) Stephen Grover Cleveland (1837–1908), 22nd and 24th President of the USA (1885–9, 1893–7), because of his rise from obscurity to power. Not being expected to win he was called **His Accidency.** He was also known as **the Perpetual Candidate** because, having served once as President, he stood again. The nickname **the Stuffed** (or **Dumb**) **Prophet** was applied when he refused to express himself publicly on some issue. When Governor of New York he was known as **Old Veto** and **Sir Veto** because he had often used one.

Man of Sedan, the: derogatory nickname for Napoleon III who capitulated to the Prussians at Sedan in the Franco-Prussian war of 1870. Also **the Prisoner of Ham** (in Surrey, where he lived in exile).

Man of Steel, the: Joseph Stalin (1879–1953), Soviet leader succeeding Lenin as head of state. The name 'Stalin' (a political pseudonym) = steel. Despite his great purges, he was more familiarly known as **Uncle Joe** — as, for example, by Winston Churchill in wartime memos and correspondence.

man-of-the-world: a sophisticated person, one who has 'been around', broad-minded.

Man on Horseback, the: see *the Bull Moose*.

Man on the Clapham Omnibus, the: the ordinary or average man, the man-in-the-street, particularly when his point of view is sought by the Courts. He was first evoked in 1903 by Lord Bowen when hearing a case of negligence: 'We must ask ourselves what the man on the Clapham omnibus would think.' Quite why he chose that particular route, we shall never know, but the present 77A to Clapham Junction (1984) does pass through Whitehall and Westminster, thus providing a link between governors and governed. There is evidence to suggest that the 'Clapham omnibus' had already become a figure of speech in the nineteenth century.

Man on the Wedding Cake, the: Governor Thomas E. Dewey of New York (1902–71), American Republican whose challenge to President Truman in the election of 1948 was scuppered, in part, by this label being attached to him. He was one of the few men to run for President wearing a moustache or beard after 1890 (he had a moustache). The remark has been variously credited to Harold Ickes and Ethel Barrymore but was given currency by Alice Roosevelt Longworth. She told William Safire: 'The first time I heard it, Grace Hodgson Flandrau remarked, "Dewey looks like the bridegroom on the wedding cake". I thought it frightfully funny and quoted it to everyone. Then it began to be attributed to me.'
Also known as **the Boy Orator of the Platitude.**

Man They Couldn't Gag, the: Peter Wilson (d.1981), sports journalist on the *Daily Mirror*, famous for his hard-hitting style and outspoken opinions. More of a by-line than a nickname, but even so. . .

Man With the Golden Flute, the: James Galway (b.1939), Ulster-born flautist who had great success as a star soloist from the mid-1970s. A promotional tag, the phrase is clearly derived from a long line which includes *The Man With the Golden Gun*, the title of a James Bond novel by Ian Fleming, *The Man With the Golden Trumpet* (see SHOW BUSINESS STARS), and *The Man With the Golden Arm*, the 1956 film about drug addiction, based on a Nelson Algren novel.

Man With the Orchid-Lined Voice, the: Enrico Caruso

(1873−1921), Italian operatic tenor and early gramophone recording star. A promotional tag devised by his publicist, Edward L. Bernays.

Man You Love To Hate, the: see FILM STARS.

Marg of Arg, the: see GOSSIP COLUMN NICKNAMES.

Mark the Shark: see GOSSIP COLUMN NICKNAMES.

Marmite Train, the: see 'PRIVATE EYE' NICKNAMES.

Martha: a housewifely woman, as was Martha, sister of Lazarus and Mary (probably Mary Magdalene: the identification of Marys in the New Testament is sometimes obscure). While Mary attended adoringly to Jesus, her sister got on with the housework − 'distracted with much serving'. Martha complained to Jesus − 'Tell her then to help me' − but Jesus defended Mary (*Luke*, 10: 38−42).

MARX BROTHERS, THE: Each member of the famous American family of comedians who appeared on stage and in films used a name other than the one he was born with. The nicknames were acquired at a poker game in approximately 1918:

> Leonard (1886−1961) became **Chico**;
> Adolph (1888−1964) became **Harpo** (he played the harp);
> Julius (1890−1977) became **Groucho**;
> Milton (1897−1977) became **Gummo** (though he left the act early on)
> Herbert (1901−79) became **Zeppo** (though he also left in due course).

Harpo commented: 'Those handles stuck from the moment they were fastened on us. Now it's like we'd never had any other names.'

Master, the: (1) D. W. Griffith (1873−1948), pioneer US film director.

(2) W. Somerset Maugham (1874−1965), novelist and playwright, noted especially for his short stories.

(3) Sir Noel Coward (1899–1973), actor, writer and wit. Known thus throughout the theatrical profession and beyond, from the 1940s on, but not to those who knew him. Coward professed not to like his nickname (perhaps because it had already been associated with Maugham) and – when asked to explain it – replied, 'Oh, you know, jack of all trades, master of none. . . '

Master of the Rolls, the: see BOXERS.

Maximum John: Judge John Sirica (b.1904), chief judge of the US District Court for Washington DC 1971–4, who achieved international fame through his participation in the Watergate prosecutions of 1973–4, because of his reputation for awarding the stiffest penalties.

Mayfair Mercs: see *Sloane Ranger*.

Maypole, the: besides being a long-standing nickname for a tall, thin person it was especially applied to Ehrengard Melusina von der Schulenburg (1667–1743), German mistress of George I, who was made Duchess of Kendal. She followed George to England and he bestowed several British and Irish titles on her, but the British public gave her only this one.

Melons: see GOSSIP COLUMN NICKNAMES.

merry Andrew: a jester, clown, from the assistant to a 'quack' doctor who fooled around on fairgrounds to attract attention. A theory is that it commemorates Andrew Boorde (or Borde), an eccentric physician, formerly a monk, who died in 1549. He travelled extensively, wrote about his journeys and the countries he visited, as well as about diet. He was said to have practised at country fairs. Several jest-books are credited to him, perhaps wrongly. He was imprisoned for keeping prostitutes in his house. (In the sixteenth and seventeenth centuries, a 'jest' meant a story, from Old French *geste* – epic poems were *chansons de geste* – and Latin *gesta*, deed or exploit. English jest-books contained light-hearted stories, and the word took on a humorous connotation.)

Merry Monarch, the: Charles II (1630–85), because of his own light-hearted character (although seriously inclined towards the arts and invention, and tolerant in religion) and the relaxation of the Restoration years in contrast with the Puritan restrictions of Cromwell's time. John Wilmot, 2nd Earl of Rochester, who was adept at writing amorous poems and rude verse, satirised Charles and his mistresses and described him as 'A merry monarch, scandalous and poor'. As a child, Charles was nicknamed **the Black Boy** because of his dark colouring, a fact that surprised his mother, Henrietta Maria.

Also known as **Old Rowley**, a nickname having two explanations — one being that it came from the name of his favourite stallion in the royal stud at Newmarket (with reference to the king's own sexual prowess), the other that it was based on the ancient legend of the two stalwart knights, Roland and Oliver, who exchanged blow for blow, hence the phrase 'a Roland for an Oliver'. The latter meaning would seem appropriate — England having found a Roland (Rowley) in exchange for an Oliver (Cromwell) — though far-fetched.

See also *the Last Man*.

Merry Widow hat: a large hat festooned with feathers, as worn by Lily Elsie in the musical play, *The Merry Widow*. It fascinated the ladies, but annoyed men sitting behind one in a theatre or encountering such on a crowded pavement. 'Merry Widow Hat Danger. Worse Than Sweep's Brush says Solicitor': headlines in the *Evening Chronicle*, Manchester, 1907.

Methodists: nickname given in 1729 to members of the 'holy club' at Oxford University and honourably adopted, becoming an identification for a religious movement, the word arising from the strict regularity of bible study and worship by John and Charles Wesley, George Whitefield and other undergraduates — the methodical way in which they observed their principles. Wesleyan Methodism began with John in 1744, although both he and Charles remained in the Church of England, the movement not becoming a separate denomination until 1795.

Micawber, a: an (often feckless) optimist, as was Wilkins Micawber, memorable character in Dickens's *David Copperfield*. Despite his penury and failure of his schemes he was always confident that something good would 'turn up', and his wife loyally supported him.

Michigan Assassin, the: see BOXERS.

Milk Snatcher: see *the Iron Lady*.

Mill Boy of the Slashes, the: Henry Clay (1777–1852) US Congressman. His boyhood chores in Virginia had included driving a donkey loaded with bags of meal from a local mill to his home in the slashes (= low, marshy ground). He became known also as **the Great Pacificator** for his eloquent support of the Missouri Compromise in 1820. By 1843 he joined the ranks of those called **the Great Commoner** and by 1850 he was **the Great Compromiser** for introducing a series of measures designed to resolve the slavery issue and avoid civil war.

Miss: in its nickname form this contraction of 'Mistress' evolved from a seventeenth-century prostitute or 'kept woman' to a Victorian and Edwardian naughty or precocious girl, and has now been absorbed into the proper word 'mistress' (which itself had a respectable – and often poetic – beginning), meaning concubine. In his *Diary* for 9 January 1662, John Evelyn refers to an actress's last appearance on the stage, 'she being taken to be the Earl of Oxford's Miss (as at that time they began to call lewd women)'. A broadsheet of the time defines the word: 'A miss is a new name which the civility of this age bestows on one that our unmannerly ancestors called whore and strumpet. A certain help mate for a gentleman instead of a wife; serving either for prevention of the sin of marrying, or else a little side pillow to render the yoke of matrimony more easy.' (Quoted from *Grub Street Stripped Bare* by Philip Pinkus, Constable, 1968.)

Miss Frigidaire: Chris Evert (later Mrs Lloyd), American tennis player, who first won the Wimbledon women's singles championship in 1974 and went on to win it twice more; noted for her unruffled — and usually unsmiling — style. Reporting on her losing to Billie Jean King in the semifinal of 1975, David Gray in the *Guardian*, 3 July, wrote: 'As we watched her (Mrs King) wearing down Miss Evert, destroying the superfine accuracy of the cold girl from Florida, we were conscious again that Mrs King is the most remarkable of post-war champions. . . How could Miss Evert, the fair Miss Frigidaire, prim and accurate, hope to counter (such) a player. . . ?' (Mrs King paid tribute elsewhere to Miss Evert's warmth off-court and her sense of humour.)

Miss Lillian: Mrs Lillian Carter (1898—1983), mother of President Jimmy Carter. Not backward in coming forward, Mrs Carter held forth on various topics and was occasionally sent on official business by her son. Her nickname betokens her origins in the South. A spoof *Punch* column of her musings called her 'Miz' Lillian.

mob, the: contraction of *mobile vulgus* (fickle crowd) and invented as a nickname by members of the Green Ribbon Club around 1680 who incited public anti-Catholic demonstrations with 'pope-burning' bonfires. Also as **the Mob:** a gang controlling organised crime in the USA.

MOG: see *the Grand Old Man*.

mohocks: eighteenth-century gangs of well-to-do ruffians, especially in London, named after the Mohawk Indians, rampaging in the streets, assaulting pedestrians, sometimes overturning coaches. Steele in *The Spectator*, No. 324, 1711, gives horrifying details of the behaviour of what he calls 'the Mohock club' and says:

> An outrageous ambition of doing all possible hurt to their fellow-creatures is the great cement of their assembly, and the only qualification required in their members. In order to exert this principle in its full strength and perfection, they take care to drink themselves to a pitch that is beyond the possibility of attending to any motions of reason or humanity. . . Some are knocked down, others stabbed, others cut and carbonaded. To put the watch to a total

rout, and mortify some of those inoffensive militia, is reckoned a *coup-d'eclat*.

These gangsters were also called 'hawkubites'.

Moll Cut-Purse: Mary Frith, a seventeenth-century highway lady who often dressed as a man, and even held up General Fairfax on Hounslow Heath. She made a small fortune out of crime and was able to buy herself out of Newgate. She died of drink, aged 75. She is commemorated in Samuel Butler's *Hudibras* (first published in 1663, the last 1678), with a change of vowel for the sake of rhyme:

> A bold virago, stout and tall,
> As Joan of France, or English Mall.

Molotov cocktail: V. M. Molotov (b.1890), former Russian revolutionary and underground fighter who became Foreign Minister of the USSR (1939–46). He gave his name to an improvised anti-tank device beloved of the British Home Guard which adopted the nickname early in the Second World War. A bottle was filled with petrol and topped with a fuse (like a firework), and when thrown against a tank the blazing liquid was supposed to spread, causing delay if not injury to the enemy.

Monks of Medmenham Abbey, the: satirical nickname for a group of dissipated young men in the early eighteenth century who met at the Thames-side home of their leader, Sir Francis Dashwood: they called themselves Franciscans after him. They were also known as 'the Hell-Fire Club' which Boswell described as 'riotous and profane'. Lord Sandwich and John Wilkes were members, sharing Dashwood's violent and wanton youth. Dashwood (1708–81) became Chancellor of the Exchequer.

Monty: Bernard Law Montgomery, 1st Viscount Montgomery of Alamein (1887–1976), really the first British general to use the promotional techniques of an American politician to secure the respect of his men and the public at large. His victory at El Alamein (1942) turned the tide of the Second World War in North Africa. After commanding ground forces in the 1944 invasion of Normandy he presided over the German surrender in 1945.

moonlighters: those who pack up their goods and silently move away by night, to avoid paying rent or other debts, hence the colloquialism 'moonlight flit'.

moonrakers: foolish yokels, extension of a Wiltshire folk-tale about the moon's reflection in the village pond being mistaken for a cheese, and their grappling for it.

moon's men: thieves and highwaymen operating at night. Falstaff says to Prince Henry in *I King Henry IV*, I:ii: 'For we that take purses go by the moon', and the prince plays with the words, remarking that 'the fortune of us that are the moon's men doth ebb and flow like the sea, being governed as the sea is, by the moon'.

morocco men: touts and sub-agents for eighteenth- and early nineteenth-century state lotteries who went about the country with impressive books bound in red leather in which speculators' names were entered: a receipt was given which did not always count for much. There was a flourishing business for contractors who bought tickets in bulk, at a discount, and sold them in shares. You could buy a ticket for £15 (with a chance of winning £20,000) or a share in a ticket for as little as three shillings, 'to afford' as one advertisement put it, 'a fair and legal opportunity for persons in every station in life to adventure upon a secure, advantageous and permanent foundation'.

morrison: an indoor air raid shelter recommended by the government in the Second World War, named after Herbert Stanley Morrison (1888–1965) when he was Home Secretary and Minister of Home Security, 1940–5. He became Baron Morrison of Lambeth.

Mother: see *the Iron Lady*.

Mouth, the: (1) Muhammad Ali. See BOXERS.
(2) Mrs Martha Mitchell (1918–76), wife of the US Attorney-General, John Mitchell. Suspicious of her husband's involve-

ment in the Watergate conspiracy she took to ringing up journalists. Although considered a liability at the time, she was vindicated.

(3) John McEnroe. See *Superbrat*.

Mr and Mrs Mole: see GOSSIP COLUMN NICKNAMES.

Mr Clean: a fairly generally applied nickname, taken from an American household cleanser, but examples of its use include: (1) Pat Boone (b.1934), US pop singer and film actor, noted for his clean image (also known as **Mr Toothpaste**) and habits (he would never agree to kiss girls in films).

(2) John Lindsay (b.1921), Mayor of New York City (1965–73) (also known as **Batman**).

(3) Elliot Richardson (b.1920), US Attorney-General who resigned in 1973 rather than agree to the restrictions President Nixon was then placing on investigations into the Watergate affair.

Mr Five Per Cent: Calouste Gulbenkian (1869–1955), Turkish-born oil millionaire and philanthropist. His share of the Turkish Petroleum Co., prior to the First World War, was reduced from 40 to 5 per cent following an Anglo-German agreement. He reckoned, however, that it was better to have a small slice of a big cake than a big slice of a small cake.

Mr Fix-It: see GOSSIP COLUMN NICKNAMES.

Mr Nice Guy: a nickname applied to 'straight' figures (especially politicians) who are either following someone who is palpably not 'nice' (like President Gerald Ford after Richard Nixon) or who feel they need to throw off some of their virtuous image (as Presidential-challenger Senator Muskie felt in 1972 – and his aides declared, 'No more Mr Nice Guy').

Mr Pastry: see 'PRIVATE EYE' NICKNAMES.

Mr Piano: see SHOW BUSINESS STARS.

Mrs Bull: see *Brandy Nan*.

Mrs Finchley: see *the Iron Lady*.

Mrs Grundy: a censorious person, upholder of accepted morality and social convention, from Thomas Morton's comedy *Speed the Plough*, 1798, in which one of the characters frequently asks, 'What will Mrs Grundy say?'

Mrs Ogmore-Pritchard: see GOSSIP COLUMN NICK-NAMES.

Mr Strange: see POP STARS.

Mr Teazy-Weazy: Peter Raymond, London hairdresser who acquired his nickname when appearing on an early 1950s TV show called *Quite Contrary*. As he put it, he would 'teasy-weasy' the curls on models while he combed out their hair in front of the cameras.

Mr Television: Milton Berle (b.1908), US comedian who was never off the screen in the early 1950s. The first big American TV star. To fans he was known as **Uncle Miltie**; to other comedians, **the Thief of Badgags**. He also used the last nickname as part of his billing.

Mr Toothpaste: see *Mr Clean*.

Mr Whip: see *Billy Blue*.

Muddy Waters: see JAZZ MUSICIANS.

mudlarks: nineteenth-century nickname for scavengers at low tide on the Thames in London, usually children and destitute adults. Henry Mayhew in his philanthropic surveys *London Labour and the London Poor* (1851–64) referred to their insanitary plight and pathetic attempts to find scraps of coal, coins or anything they could sell, from nails to crockery. They floundered knee-deep in mud, bare-footed, wearing ragged clothes, and frozen in winter.

Muggsy Spanier: see JAZZ MUSICIANS.

Muscadins: early nineteenth-century Parisian fops who mimicked what they thought were English dress and manners – top boots, high collars, long-tailed jackets, and carrying heavy sticks which they brandished at passers-by; and they spoke in loud, gruff voices. Byron mentioned them in *Don Juan*, viii: 'Cockneys of London! Muscadins of Paris!' ('Goddams' was an early French nickname for loud-mouthed English visitors who used this expletive.)

Mussolini: see 'PRIVATE EYE' NICKNAMES.

Myrtle Poisson: see GOSSIP COLUMN NICKNAMES.

N

Nabob of Sob, the: see POP STARS.

Namby-Pamby: Ambrose Philips (1675–1749), writer and politician whom the dramatist Henry Carey ridiculed with this nickname, playing on his name. The occasion was when Philips addressed some insipid verses to Lord Carteret's children. Carey, Pope and Swift thought his work received more attention than it deserved. Philips edited a Whig magazine, was an MP and a judge in Ireland. The nickname was adopted into the language to describe an insipid, pampered and childishly sentimental person.

Napoleon of Crime, the: see *the Queen of Crime*.

NATIONALITIES: Nicknames are bestowed on nationalities as if by common consent of other nationals, usually for convenience and with no ill intent (although there can be overtones of derision, as in the way some Australians pronounce *pom* or *pommy* for 'Brits', or the British use *frog* for Frenchman on the supposition that it is his favourite food.) A country's popular first-name for its citizens often meets requirements, and such nicknames have largely originated in travellers' tales or in the overseas service of soldiers. This selection covers most kinds:

American: **Doughboy, GI** (Services); **Yankee** ; **Uncle Sam** (USA personified).
Australian: **Aussie; Digger.**
Canadian: **Canuck,** especially those of French descent (probably from Chinook, an Indian tribe); also for a French Canadian, **Jean Baptiste**.
Dutchman: **Mynheer.**
Englishman: **Limey; Pom; Tommy** (military); **John Bull** (country personified).

Frenchman: **Frog**; **Johnny** (for the common Christian name Jean). Not so familiar in English nowadays is **Jacques Bonhomme** for a French countryman.

German: **Bosche**; **Fritz**; **Heine**; **Jerry**; **Kraut**.

Irishman: **Mick**; **Paddy**; **Pat**; **Mulligan** (mainly in USA).

Italian: **I-ty**; **Tony** (for Antonio).

New Zealander: **Kiwi**.

Pole: **Polack** (mostly in America).

Russian: **Russki**.

Scot: **Jock**; **Mac**; **Sandy**; **Sawney** (eighteenth and early nineteenth century, derived from Sandy, corruption of Alexander).

Spaniard (or Latin-American): **Spic** (the derivation is obscure, but perhaps it comes from 'Hispanic' or from 'spic and span'); **Dago** (from Spanish 'Diego', James).

Welshman: **Taffy** (from the common name *Dafydd*, David).

Naughty Nora: see GOSSIP COLUMN NICKNAMES.

nazis: members of the national socialist German workers' party, shortening of *Nationalsozialistische Deutsche Arbeiter-partei*, developed from 1920 under the leadership of Adolf Hitler and Ernst Roehm. It became the 'hate' word in Britain and, in his many speeches during the Second World War, Winston Churchill pronounced it with particular venom (as though it were 'nasty').

Nell of Old Drury (or **Sweet Nell**): Nell (or Eleanor) Gwynn (1650−87) who sold oranges around the Theatre Royal, Drury Lane, London and who was given acting parts, attracting attention for her liveliness and broad comedy − including the attention of Charles II whose mistress she became. She bore two sons by the king, and the elder was created Duke of St Albans. She seems to have been a generous and warm-hearted person, illiterate but intelligent. Pepys called her 'pretty, witty Nell' but Evelyn wrote disapprovingly of 'Mrs Nelly, as they called an impudent comedian'. Charles's death-bed request, 'Let not poor Nelly starve,' was faithfully kept by his brother, James II, who settled her debts and provided money and an estate.

New Deal Caesar, the: see *the Boss*.

Nicaraguan Firecracker, the: see GOSSIP COLUMN NICK-NAMES.

Nine Days' Queen, the: Lady Jane Grey (1537—54), daughter of the Duke of Suffolk and descendant of Henry VII, unfortunate pawn in the effort to transfer succession to the English throne from the Tudors to the Dudleys. She married Guildford Dudley, son of the Duke of Northumberland, and was proclaimed queen in 1553, but deposed nine days later and beheaded early in the following year.

Nipper: Leonard Read (b.1925), policeman — head of the Regional Crime Squads in England and Wales until 1976 and the man who helped bring the notorious Kray Brothers to justice. Because of his small stature. The Krays named a pet snake after him.

nippy: waitress at restaurants run by J. Lyons & Co., from the 1920s on — because of the nimble way they nipped between the tables?

Noble Yachtsman, the: satirical nickname given during the Crimean War to Lord Cardigan (7th Earl) (1797—1868) who spent much of his time aboard his yacht in Balaclava harbour where it was much more comfortable than in camp; but his courage was not in question when he led the Light Brigade in the famous suicidal charge against the Russian guns at Balaclava, 1854.

Noll: diminutive of Oliver and the nickname given to Oliver Goldsmith (1728—74) by his friends, among whom was David Garrick who is credited with this epitaph:

> Here lies Nolly Goldsmith, for shortness called Noll,
> Who wrote like an angel, but talked like poor Poll.

Dr Johnson admired him greatly, as did Horace Walpole who nevertheless described him as 'an inspired idiot'. Boswell speaks of his Irishness: 'It has been generally circulated and believed that he was a mere fool in conversation; but, in truth, this has been greatly exaggerated. He had, no doubt, a more than common share of that hurry of ideas which we often find in his countrymen, and which sometimes produces a laughable confusion in expressing them.'

Nonpareil, the: see BOXERS.

noovs: (or noovos): see *Sloane Ranger.*

Norwegian Wood: see *Fritz.*

Nose, the: (1) Barbra Streisand (b.1942), American singer with a famous proboscis.
(2) Barry Manilow (b.1946), ditto.

Nosey: (1) Oliver Cromwell (1599—1658) whose nose was bulbous and often red, earning the further nicknames of **Almighty Nose, Copper Nose** and **Ruby Nose.** Also known as **the Brewer** — a gibe by the Royalists from a belief that when a youth he helped his widowed mother in a brewery business — **Crum-Hell**, from the contemporary pronunciation of the surname, and **King Oliver**.
(2) 1st Duke of Wellington. See *the Iron Duke.*

Notre Dame de Sartre: see *the Beaver.*

Nun (or **Holy Maid**) **of Kent, the:** Elizabeth Barton (*c*.1506—34), a neurotic girl who claimed to have visions, before and after her admittance to a convent at Canterbury. She became involved in what was popularly called 'the king's great matter' and prophesied that Henry VIII would die a 'villain's death' if he divorced Catherine and married Anne Boleyn. She continued her treasonable warnings after the marriage, was examined before Star Chamber and 'confessed' — by pressure and torture, perhaps — and was executed with others at Tyburn.

Nye: Aneurin Bevan (1897—1960), Welsh Left-wing politician who was Minister of Health when the National Health Service was set up (1948). Affectionately so called.

O

Occupational Hazard, the: see GOSSIP COLUMN NICK-NAMES.

Oddjob: see GOSSIP COLUMN NICKNAMES.

OK Yoni: see 'PRIVATE EYE' NICKNAMES.

Ol' Blue Eyes: see *the Gov'nor*.

Old Abe: see *the Emancipator*.

Old 'Ard 'Art: see *Chug*.

Old Bill: nickname for an old soldier (not to be confused with the slang word for a policeman). Derived from a cartoon character created by Bruce Bairnsfather in the First World War, a whiskered, cheerful soldier who became the embodiment of the grumbling but irrepressible infantryman. Most famous was the drawing of Bill and a comrade taking refuge in a shell-hole, Bill saying: 'Well, if you knows of a better 'ole, go to it.' One of the first 'talkies' (pre-Jolson) was a Warner Brothers 'short' called *The Better 'Ole* with Syd Chaplin as Old Bill and synchronised war songs. 'Better 'Ole' became a catch phrase.

Old Blood 'n' Guts: George S. Patton (1885–1945), US General and Commander of the Third Army in the Second World War. A brilliantly forceful soldier, who liked to be regarded as a 'tough guy' in the best 'Wild West' tradition (he was flamboyant, and carried a pearl-handled revolver in an open holster); but he could be emotional and friendly — disliked by some, adored by others. The nickname is a tribute to his 'aggressive determination'.

Old Chapultepec/ Old Chippewa: see *Old Fuss and Feathers.*

Old Contemptibles, the: rank and file in the British Expeditionary Force which crossed the Channel in 1914 to join the French and Belgians against the German advance in the First World War. It was alleged that Kaiser Wilhelm II had described the force as 'a contemptibly little army' (referring to its size rather than its quality). The British press was then said to have mistranslated this so that it made him appear to have called the BEF a 'contemptible little army'.

The truth is that the whole episode was a propaganda ploy master-minded by the British. A fake order from the German Emperor, using the phrase, was issued by the War Office. No evidence of any similar order was ever found in German archives. The ex-Kaiser himself later denied having said any such thing.

After the war, BEF veterans who had taken the name kept contact and paraded annually until 1974 when too few remained.

Old Crock: Anthony C. McAuliffe (1898–1975), US general in the Second World War. When asked to surrender by the Germans during the Battle of the Bulge, 1944, he replied, famously: 'Nuts!' His nickname was self-inflicted in a talk to his men.

Old Dutch: a beloved wife, short for 'duchess', probably of Cockney origin. The comedian Albert Chevalier (1861–1923) spread the nickname with his song *My Old Dutch* – 'There ain't a lady living in the land as I'd swap for my dear old Dutch.'

Old Fox, the: see *the Father of His Country.*

Old Fuss and Feathers: General Winfield Scott (1786–1866), US soldier, referring to his vanity and pomposity. After battles he fought and won he was also called **Old Chippewa** and **Old Chapultepec.**

Old Glad-Eye(s): see *the Grand Old Man.*

Old Groaner, the: Harry Lillis Crosby (1904—77), American popular singer, better known by his other nickname **Bing** or (in German) **Der Bingle**. Oddly, he had rather a smooth low voice rather than a groaning one. As one of the first crooners, however, inevitably the name stuck. Also: **One-Take** for his ability to make a recording without mistakes.

Old Grog: see *Grog*.

Old Hickory: Andrew Jackson (1767—1845), US general and 7th President (1828—36), so called by his men in 1813 during a battle against Creek Indians because he proved himself 'tough as hickory' wood. To his opponents: **King Andrew**.

Old Hopalong: see 'PRIVATE EYE' NICKNAMES.

Old Kinderhook: see *the Little Magician*.

Old Man Eloquent: John Quincy Adams (1767—1848), 6th President of the USA (1825—29). He had been Boylston professor of rhetoric and oratory at Harvard University. Also the **Accidental President** because he received only thirteen of the twenty-four votes cast in the electoral college after the 1824 election. His contemporaries felt that his only getting a majority of one was an accident.

Old Nick: one of the oldest nicknames for Satan, probably brought by Viking invaders, from a Scandinavian word for a water goblin; or the Anglo-Saxons may have been responsible because of a similar Teutonic word. Also: **Old Harry, Auld Clootie, Auld Hangie, Nickie-ben, Old Scratch, Satanic Majesty, Father of Lies**, etc.

Old Nosey: see *the Iron Duke*.

Old Oyster-Eyes: see 'PRIVATE EYE' NICKNAMES.

Old Peacock: see *Tum-Tum*.

Old Pretender, the: James Francis Edward Stuart (1688—1766), son of James II and claimant to the English throne. He was supported by Louis XIV of France who regarded him as James III, but he spent his life in exile and died in Rome. Another nickname was **the Warming Pan baby**, from the anti-Jacobite rumour that he was smuggled when a baby into the bedroom of his mother (Mary of Modena — second wife of James II) in a warming pan because her own child was stillborn. His Jacobite followers were sneered at as 'Warming Pans'.

Old Public Functionary: James Buchanan (1791–1868), 15th US President (1857–61). In an address to Congress he made an appeal to end 'sectional strife' and said the appeal came from 'the heart of an old public functionary'. Also known as **the Bachelor President**, because he was.

Old Rough and Ready: Zachary Taylor (1784–1850), 12th President of the USA (1849–50) and hero of the Mexican War. He was born in Virginia but brought up on the wild Kentucky frontier and with little education. His troops gave him this nickname because of his informal dress and 'lack of military pretension'. Also: **Old Zack.**

Old Rowley: see *the Merry Monarch.*

Old Slow Hand: see POP STARS.

Old Three Stars: see *the Butcher.*

Old Timber: Sir Henry Wood (1869–1944), conductor and founder of the London Promenade Concerts. 'Timber' is an inevitable nickname for a man called Wood(s).

Old Tippecanoe: see *Tippecanoe.*

Old Turkey Neck: see *Vinegar Joe.*

Old Veto: see *the Man of Destiny.*

One and Only, the: see SHOW BUSINESS STARS.

One-Armed Bandit, the: see GOSSIP COLUMN NICKNAMES.

One-Leg Paget: Henry William Paget, 1st Marquess of Anglesey (1768—1854) who, as Lord Uxbridge, a cavalry officer, lost his right leg at Waterloo. The story goes that in the battle he suddenly exclaimed, 'By God, sir, I've lost my leg!' to which Wellington replied, 'By God, sir, so you have!' and continued his direction of hostilities. The partly severed leg was amputated, placed in a coffin and buried in a garden in the village of Waterloo.

One Night Standrew: see GOSSIP COLUMN NICKNAMES.

One-Take: (given generally to performers who avoid making mistakes when being filmed or recorded, but especially:
(1) Bing Crosby.
(2) Shirley Temple (b.1928), child film actress.
(3) Charles, Prince of Wales — as **One-Take Wales** — applied by Princess Anne. See also *Action Man* and 'PRIVATE EYE' NICKNAMES.

Oom Paul: see *Uncle Paul.*

Oomph Girl, the: see FILM STARS.

Oonter: see 'PRIVATE EYE' NICKNAMES.

Opium Eater, the: Thomas de Quincey (1785—1859), author and essayist, who led an unsettled though productive life. He acquired a taste for opium while at Oxford — taken to allay neuralgia. His *Confessions of an English Opium Eater,* 1822, introduced him to a wide public — a book of considerable literary merit as well as being self-revelatory.

Orangemen: members of the Orange Order, founded in Ulster in 1795 with the aim of maintaining the Protestant constitution. The name commemorates William of Orange, who became William III and who defeated the army of exiled James II at the Battle of the Boyne, 1690.

Orange Peel: Sir Robert Peel (1788—1850) who was Secretary for Ireland at the age of 24, and although trying to hold a balance was compelled to show Protestant bias, and later in the House of Commons led the opposition to Roman Catholic emancipation. His attitude changed, however, and in 1829 he backed the emancipation cause in a speech of more than four hours. Then he was known as **the Runaway Spartan.**

Orator Hunt: Henry Hunt (1773–1835), radical politician, prominent at public meetings, wearing the white hat of the reformer. He tried unsuccessfully to become an MP, but was not elected (for Preston) until 1830. In the meantime he had been imprisoned for conspiracy, arrested at the open-air meeting in Manchester which became known as the 'Peterloo massacre'. Later he championed women's rights and presented the first petition of this kind to Parliament.

Orchid Man: see BOXERS.

Oriana: see *Gloriana.*

Oscar: an Academy Award – in the shape of statuettes presented each year by the American Academy of Motion Picture Arts and Sciences for distinction in film acting, writing and production (since 1928). Designed by Cedric Gibbons, MGM's art director, they traditionally took their name from a comment made by Margaret Herrick, a secretary at the Academy. Seeing one *c.*1931, she declared: 'Why, it looks just like my uncle Oscar,' – i.e. Oscar Pierce, a wheat and fruit grower.

Our Ginny: Virginia Wade (b.1945), tennis player and Wimbledon women's champion.

Our Gracie: see SHOW BUSINESS STARS.

Our Marie: see SHOW BUSINESS STARS.

Our Shirl: see 'PRIVATE EYE' NICKNAMES.

Our Val: see GOSSIP COLUMN NICKNAMES.

P

Paleface: the 'White Man' in the eyes of North American Indians who, in return, were dubbed 'Redskins', according to popular fiction, the fashion set by American novelist James Fenimore Cooper.

Pam: 3rd Viscount Palmerston (1784–1865), Foreign Secretary and twice Prime Minister.

Pantomime King, the: see SHOW BUSINESS STARS.

Parrot Face: see SHOW BUSINESS STARS.

Parsley Peel: Robert Peel (1750–1830), wealthy Lancashire cotton manufacturer who inherited his father's calico-printing firm and became father of the more famous Sir Robert. This elder Robert was also an MP. One of his best-selling fabrics with a parsley pattern became very fashionable, prompting his workpeople to invent the nickname which spread to those 'in the know' in the rest of the country.

Pasionaria, La: political tag used by Dolores Ibarruri (b.1895), Spanish Communist leader at the time of the Civil War. Means 'passion-flower'.

Pasionaria of Privilege, the: see *the Iron Lady*.

Paul Pry: an inquisitive, interfering kind of person, from the comedy of that name by John Poole (1785–1872).

Peanut: see *President Peanut*.

pearlies: costermongers in the East End of London who, from about 1875, began to decorate their clothes with pearl buttons on festive occasions, a custom that grew into a tradition, with elaborate designs on suits and dresses and the election of 'pearly kings' and 'queens'. They still carry out much charitable work.

Peekaboo Girl, the: see FILM STARS.

Peeler: a policeman, named after Sir Robert Peel when he was Secretary for Ireland (1812—18) and founded the Irish Constabulary. Later, as Home Secretary in England, he instituted the Metropolitan Police Force in London and the nickname was carried with him. It was largely superseded by *Bobby*.

Peeping Tom: usually applied to a man who spies on female privacy — a voyeur — as did the tailor in Coventry when Lady Godiva rode naked through the streets. The legend is that when she pleaded with her husband Leofric to relieve the citizens of their taxes he challenged her in this fashion. After her ride on horseback with only her long hair as covering he granted her wish. In deference to her modesty the grateful townsfolk kept indoors and drew their shutters — all except Tom the tailor who took a peep, and was struck blind.

Pee-Wee Russell: see JAZZ MUSICIANS.

Pelvis, the: see *Elvis the Pelvis*.

Penny-a-liner: a freelance journalist contributing news items to the papers, his payment calculated according to the number of lines used; for many years the rate was a penny.

Pentonville 5, the: see *the Chicago 7*.

People of the Book: Jews — widely used for a long time, and even in recent years as, for example, 'What did they know of agriculture? The People of the Book were the people of the market place, not the soil . . . ' (Bernet Litvinoff, *Weizmann, Last of the Patriarchs*, 1976). The 'Book', of course, is the

Bible, but the nickname has also been applied to Moham-medans and their Koran.

Perdita: see *Fair Perdita*.

Perpetual Candidate, the: see *the Man of Destiny*.

Philosopher of Sans-Souci, the: Frederick II (1712–86), King of Prussia, better known as **Frederick the Great**. His palace near Berlin was named Sans Souci ('without care').

Phoney Quid, the: Admiral of the Fleet, Sir Dudley Pound (1877–1943), First Sea Lord during the Second World War. In the navy, anyone called Pound gets the name 'Quid' (from the slang for a pound sterling). Sir Dudley thus acquired this clever extension (from dud=phoney).

Phrasemaker, the: Woodrow Wilson (1856–1924), 28th US President (1913–21) for such utterances as, 'The world must be made safe for democracy' (1917). Also known as **the Schoolmaster** and **Professor** because of his manner — but he had been professor of jurisprudence and political economy at Princeton.

Phyllis: see POP STARS.

Picts: painted ladies, a nickname coined by Steele in *The Spectator*, No.41, 1711, from the ancient Scottish tribes who indulged in war paint. In a tirade against make-up he wrote:

The muscles of a real face sometimes swell with soft passion, sudden surprise, and are flushed with agreeable confusions . . . But the Picts behold all things with the same air, whether they are joyful or sad; the same fixed insensibility appears upon all occasions. A Pict, though she takes all that pains to invite the approach of lovers, is obliged to keep them at a certain distance; a sigh in a languishing lover, if fetched too near her, would dissolve a feature; and a kiss snatched by a forward one, might transfer the complexion of the mistress to the admirer.

Piggy: (or **the Pig**) Sir Robert Muldoon (b.1921), Prime Minister of New Zealand 1975–84, criticised as porcine in both demeanour and behaviour by his adversaries. A graffito on an Auckland bacon factory in 1981 read: 'Pigs disown Muldoon'.

Pincher: Admiral Sir William F. Martin (fl.1860), a strict disciplinarian who insisted on ratings being put under arrest ('pinched') for even minor offences. From this use it has become an inseparable nickname for anyone surnamed Martin.

Ping: see GOSSIP COLUMN NICKNAMES.

Pink Crimplene: see GOSSIP COLUMN NICKNAMES.

Pin-up Girl: one whose physical attractions merit a photograph in a magazine or calendar, so that it can be cut out and displayed for admiration.

Piranha Teeth: see 'PRIVATE EYE' NICKNAMES.

Plantagenet: nickname given to Geoffrey, Count of Anjou (1113–51) and which became the surname of a dynasty. It was said that he had a habit of wearing a sprig of broom (*planta genista*, or *genet*) in his cap, or that he planted broom. He also had the honorific of *le bel*, the handsome. His eldest son by his wife Matilda became Henry II of England, 'the first of the Plantagenets'.

Platinum Blonde, the: see FILM STARS.

Plon-Plon: Prince Napoleon Joseph Charles Paul Bonaparte (1822–91), second son of Jerome Bonaparte (a brother of Napoleon) who commanded a division in the Crimean War, soldiers' translation of *plomb-plomb*, or *craint-plomb* ('fear lead'). It was an unkind nickname given him after the Battle of Alma when his courage under fire was questioned, probably without justification.

Plum: (1) Sir Pelham Francis Warner (1873–1963), cricketer and cricket writer, always known thus.

(2) Sir Pelham (P.G.) Wodehouse (1881—1975), novelist and creator of Jeeves and Bertie Wooster. Both, clearly, from a contraction of 'Pelham'.

Plumed Knight, the: James G. Blaine (1830—93), defeated candidate in the 1884 US Presidential Election. In a flowery presentation speech at the 1876 Republican convention, Robert Ingersoll said: 'Like an armed warrior, like a plumed knight, James G. Blaine marched down the halls of the American Congress and threw his shining lance full and fair against the brazen forehead of the defamers of our country and the maligners of his honour . . . '

Pocket Dictator, the: Englebert Dollfuss (1892—1934), Austrian statesman, because of his small stature. When he became Chancellor in 1932 he tried to unite all parties against the Nazi menace, but was assassinated two years later.

Pom: (or **Pommy**) Australian nickname for an Englishman (sometimes for other residents of the UK) and used to a much lesser extent in New Zealand. There have been many attempts to explain the derivation (e.g. from pomegranate/immigrant, from POME — Prisoner of Mother England, or from POHM — Prisoner of Her Majesty), but it is probably a simple corruption of Tom or Tommy. It was used in fairly friendly fashion until after the Second World War and the upsurge of Australian nationalism; then it often took on a derogatory tone, as in 'Ten Pound Poms' — those British emigrants who entered the country under the assisted-passage scheme — and 'Pommy bastards'.

poodle-faker: a womaniser, from Anglo-Indian and Services' parlance of the early twentieth century. Presumably the idea is that the man imitates a lap dog in some manner.

Popeye: see GOSSIP COLUMN NICKNAMES.

Pops: see *Satchmo*.

POP STARS: Some pop stars have manufactured nicknames

for themselves (see 'Chubby' Checker below) and others have derived their stagenames from nicknames (see 'Sting' and 'Mr Strange'). Otherwise:

Beryl: John Reid, manager of Elton John — one of a group of female nicknames, as in *Phyllis* and *Sharon* below.

Boy George: George Alan O'Dowd, whose stage name derived from a nickname, became a successful singer with the group Culture Club from 1983. As he dressed as a woman, his name was a useful indication of gender.

Chubby Checker: Originator of the Twist. His real name is Ernest Evans. His stage name was contrived to parallel 'Fats' Domino, to whom he bears a resemblance (Chubby=Fats, Checker=Domino).

Fats Domino: Antoine Domino. His first record in 1948 was entitled 'The Fat Man'.

Golden Boy: (1) Frankie Avalon, also known as **the Young Sinatra** (2) Paul Anka.

Golden Girl of Pop, the: Kathy Kirby.

King of Glam Rock, the: Gary Glitter.

King of Rock 'n' Roll, the: see sep. entry for *Elvis the Pelvis*.

King of the Calypso, the: Harry Belafonte.

Leather Lungs: Elaine Page.

Little Miss Dynamite: Brenda Lee.

Liver Lips: Bob Geldof. His nickname at school.

Mr Clean: see sep. entry.

Mr Strange: Stephen Harrington. Nicknamed 'Mr Strange' by a postman for his habit of wearing make-up and spiky hair, he took this as his stage name.

Old Slow Hand: Eric Clapton, rock guitarist. Because of his distinctive twangy guitar sound.

Phyllis: Rod Stewart, rock singer.

Prince of Wails, the: Johnnie Ray. Also known as **the Cry Guy** and **the Nabob of Sob.** He had an emotional way of singing.

Sharon: Elton John.

Sting: Gordon Sumner, lead singer with The Police. He was nicknamed 'Sting' at the age of sixteen for his habit of wearing a wasp-striped T-shirt. It became his stage name.

See also *Elvis the Pelvis, the Forces' Sweetheart, the Gov'nor, and the Old Groaner.*

Popski's Private Army: a small British unit under Lt-Col Vladimir Peniakoff which carried out raids and reconnaissance in North Africa, and later in Italy, in the Second World War. Peniakoff (of Russian parents, educated in England) was a volunteer in the Long Range Desert Group operating behind enemy lines.

pot-hunters: Services' nickname (especially in the RAF) for those considered to set their sights on awards and decorations — these called 'gongs', or 'pots'.

Pot(t)awatomie Giant, the: see BOXERS.

pre-Raphaelites: the 'brotherhood' of artists formed in 1848 by William Holman Hunt, J. E. Millais and D. G. Rossetti and joined by F. G. Stephens, T. Woolner, W. H. Deverell and J. Collinson to establish a simpler and more naturalistic style of painting than was in vogue at the time. The name — which might be thought to indicate that they were emulating painters earlier than Raphael — was more of a reflection that they thought Raphael over-praised. Their pictures — for the most part — were characterised by high colours and minute detail. They at first agreed to sign their pictures PRB. They shocked most of the critics, except Ruskin who gave encouragement.

President de Facto, the: see *the Fraud.*

President Peanut: (or **Jiminy Peanuts** or simply **Peanut**) Jimmy Carter (b.1924), 39th US President (1977−81). About the only things anybody knew about him when he became President were that he had been Governor of Georgia and that his family ran a prosperous peanut business. When running for President he was dubbed **Jimmy Who?** as few had ever heard of him.
See also 'PRIVATE EYE' NICKNAMES.

Pretty Fanny: Arthur J. Balfour (later Lord Balfour) (1848−

1930), Conservative Prime Minister (1902—5). Kenneth Young comments in his biography (G. Bell & Sons, 1963):

> There *was* a feminine streak in his character; it emerged again at Cambridge in his predilection for blue china in his rooms. This seemed to some of his fellow-undergraduates rather affected and, because he was also somewhat fastidious in his habits, he received the nickname . . . When he first entered the House of Commons, observers thought there was about him 'a distinct flavour of effeminacy'. Nor did he ever marry. But there was never any suggestion of the homosexual about Balfour.

Pretty Thing: see GOSSIP COLUMN NICKNAMES.

Prez: see JAZZ MUSICIANS.

Prime Irish Lad, the: see BOXERS.

Prime Minister of Mirth, the: see SHOW BUSINESS STARS.

Prince of Macaronies: George Bussy, 4th Earl of Jersey (1735—1805), holder of several offices at the court of George III and noted for his elegance of manner and dress.

Prince of Showmen, the: see SHOW BUSINESS STARS.

Prince of Wails, the: see POP STARS.

Princess of Parallelograms: Byron's nickname for Anna Isabella (Annabella) Milbanke, whom he married in 1815, because of her interest in mathematics. Their marriage was disastrous.

Princess Tom: see GOSSIP COLUMN NICKNAMES.

Principe, Il: Sir Peter Hall (b.1930), director of the National Theatre — for his empire-building activities, perhaps with a Machiavellian tinge?

Prinny (or **Prinney**): George IV (1762—1830) when Prince Regent (1811—20). The nickname occurs frequently in the papers of Thomas Creevey who took it from his step-daughters, the Misses Ord, who saw much of the Prince in childhood.

When Prince of Wales he had adopted the name **Florizel** in his affair with Mrs Robinson (*Fair Perdita*), the actress who attracted his attention in Garrick's production of *The Winter's Tale*, 1778. It was a passing, though passionate, episode in his amorous career, not comparable with his later love for Maria Fitzherbert whom he secretly married and whose good influence on him lasted until he became Prince Regent, despite his selfishness. The Prince's several amours and succession of mistresses were public property, and there was little reticence in criticism of him; for example, Pierce Egan's *The Mistress of Royalty, or the loves of Florizel and Perdita*.

As King, he was called **Fum the Fourth** by Byron in *Don Juan*, xi:

> Where's Whitbread? Romilly? Where's George the Third?
> Where is his will? (That's not so soon unriddled).
> And where is 'Fum the Fourth', our 'royal bird'?
> Gone down, it seems, to Scotland to be fiddled
> Unto by Sawney's violin, we have heard.

By those more prone to flattery, he was known as **the First Gentleman of Europe.**

Prisoner of Ham, the: see *the Man of Sedan*.

Prisoner of Spandau, the: British press nickname for Rudolph Hess (b.1894) who became Hitler's deputy. He surprised the world in May 1941 by flying to Scotland, ostensibly to try and arrange a separate peace between Germany and Britain. By the end of the war his mind seemed to be unbalanced, and he sat through the war crimes trial at Nuremburg as if not understanding what was going on. He was condemned in 1946 to life imprisonment and in the 1970s efforts to obtain his release from Spandau gaol (in Berlin) began on humanitarian grounds. These efforts were repeatedly rebuffed by his Soviet gaolers.

private eye: a private detective, Americanism quickly adopted in Britain, popularised in films and television programmes. The expression is said to have originated from the eye motif on an advertisement for the first Pinkerton detective agency in Chicago, 1850. However, it may be no more than a contraction of 'Private I(nvestigator)'.

'PRIVATE EYE' NICKNAMES: The British satirical fortnightly *Private Eye* was first published in 1962. A mixture of parodies of current events (in newspaper style), sometimes unfounded gossip, and serious investigative reporting, the *Eye* has given rise to numerous nicknames. Some of these have been acquired from elsewhere (so many of the following nicknames are interchangeable with those in GOSSIP COLUMN NICKNAMES) while others are entirely the *Eye's* own. Many readers come to find it impossible to call public figures by their actual names, so pervasive are the *Eye* nicknames. This is a selection drawn mainly from the late 1970s and early 80s:

Badger: Ron Hall, a journalist.

Baillie Vass: (or **the Baillie**) the Earl of Home, later Sir Alec Douglas-Home, later Lord Home. In the early days of the magazine it carried a misprint from a Scottish newspaper which had transposed photo captions. Under the Earl of Home's picture were the words 'Baillie Vass' and the name stuck.

Baldilocks: Gerald Kaufman, prominent Labour politician, notable for lack of hirsuteness.

Beast, the: Anthony Haden-Guest (also **the Uninvited Guest**), a journalist.

Biggles: Sir Max Aitken, newspaper proprietor (son of Lord Beaverbrook) and Battle of Britain pilot.

Biglips: Mick Jagger, a singer.

Blessed Arnold, the: see *Two-Dinners* below.

Boy David, the: David Steel, leader of the Liberal Party, because of his relative youth and youthful looks.

Brenda: HM The Queen. All Royal Family nicknames are designed to show that it is, in essence, a suburban family. See also *Lillibet*.

Brian: HRH The Prince of Wales. See also *Action Man* and *One-Take*.

Bubonic Plagiarist, the: see *Gypsy Dave* below.

Charlie's Aunt: see *Yvonne* below.

Cheryl: HRH The Princess of Wales. See also *Dutch*.

Dame Harold: Harold Evans, sometime editor of the *Sunday Times* and *The Times*. So dubbed by the Earl of Arran for his supposed resemblance to Dame Edith Evans. He does not like the name.

Dirty Digger, the: (or just **the Digger**) Rupert Murdoch, thrustful Australian-born international newspaper tycoon. ('Digger' has long been applied to Australian and New Zealand soldiers, especially during the World Wars, and used as a form of address among Australians, like 'cobber'.)

Doctor, the: Jonathan Miller, Renaissance man and surely the equal of Dr Johnson in conversation, but also a medical doctor somewhere along the line.

Dr Death: David Owen, Labour minister and a founder of the SDP — because he was a medical doctor and because of his dark looks.

Flame-Haired Temptress, the: (or **Titian-Haired . . .**) Audrey Slaughter, a journalist.

Gladys: Mary Wilson, wife of former Prime Minister Harold Wilson, was spared the use of her real name in the long-running feature 'Mrs Wilson's Diary'.

Goldenballs: Sir James Goldsmith, industrialist. *Private Eye* was involved in prolonged litigation over comments it had made about Sir James, around the time he set up a short-lived new magazine called *NOW!* (re-christened *Talbot!* by the magazine because Chrysler motor cars had just been renamed Talbot). **Sir Jams,** as he was also called because of his grocery business, gave rise to **the Marmite Train** (cf. 'Gravy Train') of journalists who were persuaded to work for him for lots of money. The name 'Goldenballs', incidentally, was used as an abusive nickname as long ago as the Domesday Book. As 'gildyn ballokes' it lasted until the fourteenth century.

Greatest Living Englishman, the: Nigel Dempster, gossip-columnist, who has contributed to the *Eye* pseudony-mously, as part of 'Grovel'. He promoted himself thus. Perhaps the term had been most used previously regarding Sir Winston Churchill, though there had been some ironic use in connection with Cyril Connolly, the writer and critic.

Grocer, the: Edward Heath. A notable *Eye* coinage. Partly because of the future Prime Minister's dealings in Resale Price Maintenance legislation and his negotiations for British entry to the EEC, but also partly because of his social background.

Gypsy Dave: David Frost (also **the Bubonic Plagiarist** – a term coined by Jonathan Miller).

Herr Schidt: Helmut Schmidt, when West German Chancellor.

Jaybotham: Peter Jay, who was appointed Ambassador to the United States by his father-in-law (Prime Minister James Callaghan), ousting the incumbent Sir Peter Ramsbotham.

Kaiser Bill: William Davis, a former editor of *Punch*, believed to have German origins. (Cf. sep. entry.)

Keith: HRH The Duke of Edinburgh.

Ken Leninspart: Ken Livingstone, GLC leader (see also *Red Ken*). From 'Lenin' coupled with 'Dave Spart' (the *Eye*'s all-purpose Left-winger).

Lady Forkbender: Marcia Williams, Harold Wilson's private secretary was ennobled in 1974 and took the name Lady Falkender. This was shortly after a man called Uri Geller had demonstrated an unusual power to bend spoons. At times, the good lady seemed to have a similar capacity.

Lady Magnesia Freelove: Lady Antonia Fraser, the writer, just as she was leaving her first husband, eventually re-emerging as Lady Antonia Pinter.

Lord Clark of Civilisation: when Kenneth Clark, the art historian who presented the TV series *Civilisation*, was created a Life Peer – taking the title Lord Clark of Saltwood – he was given this more appropriate nickname. See also *K* as a sep. entry.

Lord Gnome: is the name of the absentee proprietor of the magazine – based loosely on Lord Beaverbrook – but it is often applied to the editor, Richard Ingrams.

Lord Porn: Lord Longford. See sep. entry.

Lord Whelks: Lord Matthews, newspaper proprietor

(among other things), of somewhat London origins. His son, Ian, is known as **Winkle.**

Mad Monk, the: Sir Keith Joseph. In the early stages of Mrs Thatcher's government, Sir Keith was believed to be something of an *Eminence Grise* if not actually on a par with the original *Mad Monk*. Also: **Sir Sheath** — when he was Health Secretary, he was believed to have advocated greater self-control in sexual matters (or greater use of contraceptives) among the lower classes.

Mr Pastry: Sir Monty Finniston, former Chairman of British Steel, after a ramshackle children's TV character of the 1950s.

Mussolini: Clive Irving, newspaper executive, who once had a hand in the proposed publication of Mussolini's diaries (later found to be forgeries), which the *Eye's* nickname for him never allows anyone to forget.

OK Yoni: Yoko Ono, widow of John Lennon.

Old Hopalong: Ronald Reagan, US President and former film actor, after Hopalong Cassidy, the fictional film cowboy. See also sep. entry under *the Gipper.*

Old Oyster-Eyes: Lord (William) Whitelaw, Tory politician. Because he looks like that. See also *Wobbling Willie.*

Oonter: Hunter Davies, a writer.

Our Shirl: see *Shirl the Pearl* below.

Piranha Teeth: Jocelyn Stevens, newspaper executive — for his management style rather than because of any dentures he may have.

Scotch-Eggs: Henry Keswick, a millionaire former pro-prietor of *The Spectator.*

Sherpa, the: Anthony Howard, Nepalese-like journalist.

Shirl the Pearl: (also **Our Shirl**) Shirley Williams, SDP politico.

Shit of Persia, the: the Shah of Iran. He was very upset about this.

Sid Yobbo: Derek Jameson, editor of various popular newspapers including the *News of the World*. Has an engagingly down-market manner.

Slicker of Wakefield, the: John Poulson, Yorkshire archi-tect, gaoled for conspiring to corrupt.

Smoothiechops: Roy Jenkins, Labour minister then

founder of the SDP. Later **Woy,** because of his inability to pwonounce the letter 'r'.

Stevarse: Norman St John Stevas MP.

Tarzan: Michael Heseltine, prominent Tory politician. Would be a suitable nickname if only because of his tallness and blond hair (hence also **Brilliantine**), but was acquired because of an incident in 1976 when (according to some versions) he waved aloft the House of Commons mace in order to protect it.

Toadthrush: President Carter, for no discernible reason. See also *President Peanut*.

Two-Dinners: Lord Goodman, top lawyer, who always looks as if he has had about ten. Also: **the Blessed Arnold.**

Usurer of the Valleys, the: Sir Julian Hodge, target of an *Eye* campaign.

Wislon: Harold Wilson, the victim of a prolonged misprint (in the same way as the *Guardian* is invariably called the *Grauniad*.) See also *the Houdini of Politics*.

Worzel Gummidge: Michael Foot, when leader of the Labour Party, because of his disshevelled appearance. The children's stories about a scarecrow with this name had recently been dramatised for TV.

Yvonne: HRH The Princess Margaret. She herself may have coined another epithet — **Charlie's Aunt** — which, indeed, she is.

Prof, the: Frederick Lindeman (1886–1957), Professor of Experimental Philosophy at Oxford University, later created Viscount Cherwell. He became Churchill's chief scientific adviser before and during the Second World War. (But a nickname frequently applied to anyone of an academic bent.)

Professor: (1) Woodrow Wilson. See *the Phrasemaker*.
(2) Jimmy Edwards. See SHOW BUSINESS STARS.

Prosperity's Advance Agent: William McKinley (1843–1901), 25th US President (1897–1901), because a period of prosperity did, indeed, follow close upon his election.

Public Enemy No 1: popularly applied to any bogey-man. The term 'Public Enemy' was introduced in 1923 by Frank

Loesch of Chicago's Crime Commission in an attempt to dispel any romantic aura from around the likes of Al Capone. The FBI's first list of the Ten Most Wanted Men in the early 1930s was headed by the bank robber and killer, John Dillinger, though the other names were not in numbered order. Variants have included: **Public Stomach No 1** for Raymond Postgate, founder of the *Good Food Guide* and **Public Anemone No 1,** self-applied by Beverley Nichols, the writer.

Pucelle, La: see *the Maid of Orleans.*

Pug: General Sir Hastings (later Lord) Ismay (1887–1965), because he looked like one.

Pussyfoot Johnson: W. E. Johnson (1862–1945), American law-enforcement officer in Indian territory who pursued law-breakers, especially in gambling saloons, with stealth and persistence. He was especially anti-alcohol and worked tirelessly for prohibition, in later years lecturing all over the country. His nickname was transferred to advocates of temperance or complete abstinence from alcohol. 'Pussyfooting' then came to mean any weak, evasive activity.

Q

quack: itinerant drug seller at fairs who 'quacked' forth the praise of his wares, a shortening of 'quacksalver' which produced the nickname and from which we get 'quack doctor', a pretender to knowledge of medicine, or at least an unconventional one. The word probably came from the German *quaken* or the Dutch *kwakken*, to croak (like a duck).

Quaker Poet, the: (1) Bernard Barton (1784−1849), a bank clerk who attained some distinction with his verses, friend of Lamb and Southey.
(2) John Greenleaf Whittier (1807−92), American poet whose work is perhaps best known in Britain in hymnals.

Quakers: nickname of derision given to followers of George Fox (1624−91) in his early itinerant preaching days and which the movement retained − as it still does − after it adopted the title of the Religious Society of Friends. When Fox was charged with blasphemy at Derby in 1650 he told the magistrate, 'Tremble and quake at the name of the Lord!', to which Bennett (the magistrate) replied, 'You quake, do you? Quakers, eh?' The public seized the name to identify this new and vigorous group (which became the largest dissenting sect, and which in later years has had a social influence far outweighing its comparatively small membership).

Queen Dick: Richard Cromwell (1626−1712), son of Oliver, given during his short reign after his father's death, because of his timidity and inability to cope with events, as well as the rumours of homosexuality − probably unfounded. His friends nicknamed him **King Dick,** and when he gave up the protectorate he was called **Tumbledown Dick.** He sought a quiet life in Paris under the name of John Clarke, and on return to England he died in obscurity.

Queen of Crime, the: (1) Agatha Christie (1891–1976), the detective novelist and playwright – a promotional tag, associating her with crimes she wrote about rather than committed (as opposed to Conan Doyle's tag of **the Napoleon of Crime** for his character Count Moriarty – re-applied to T. S. Eliot's Macavity the Mystery Cat).
   (2) P. D. (Phyllis) James (b.1920), the crime novelist, when the promotional tag was passed on to her in a *Newsweek* review.

Queen of the Halls/ Music Hall: see SHOW BUSINESS STARS.

Queen Sarah: Sarah Churchill (née Jennings) (1660–1744), Duchess of Marlborough, because of her influence at the court of Queen Anne. She played an important part in her husband's career, until she fell from grace. While on terms of close friendship with the queen they called each other Mrs Freeman and Mrs Morley.

Queer Hardie: (James) Keir Hardie (1856–1915), a founder and chairman of the Independent Labour Party, a Labour member of parliament and a man of great integrity and character; a play on his name and in recognition of his quirks, such as wearing a cloth cap. *Punch*, 3 July 1912, called him 'Don't Keir Hardie'. Bernard Shaw described him as 'the damndest natural aristocrat in the House of Commons'.

quisling: a traitor, fifth columnist, a word adopted into the language from Vidkun Quisling, former Minister of Defence in Norway who supported the invasion of his country by the Germans in 1940. He headed a puppet government under the Nazi occupation. After the German defeat he was tried and executed in 1945.

R

Rabbi of Bray, the: Leon Brittan (b.1939), Conservative politician — by way of reference to his Jewishness and to the Vicar of Bray of the sixteenth century (celebrated in song) who backed whichever faction was ahead at the time.

Rab's Boys: a team working under R. A. Butler to reform the Conservative Party after its defeat in the post-war election of 1945 and moulding it into a strong opposition. It prepared a programme for industry, with the aim of full employment, co-operation between workers and employers, wages related to productivity, greater security for workers; free enterprise but accepting some nationalisation. Controls were criticised and lower taxation urged. In the Conservative victory of 1951 Butler became Chancellor of the Exchequer.

raglan: another eponymous nickname, this one for a style of loose coat, sleeves extending to the neck without seams on the shoulders, as worn by Lord Raglan (1788—1855) who fought at Waterloo (and lost a hand) and who commanded the British forces in the Crimea, where he died of dysentery.

Rail Splitter, the: see *the Emancipator*.

Railway King, the: George Hudson (1800—71), a farmer's son who became a draper in York and mayor of the city, an MP and founder of a banking company. He was actively concerned in railway development, made a fortune but lost that and his reputation by over-speculation and questionable accountancy.

Randy Andy: see GOSSIP COLUMN NICKNAMES.

Ranji: nickname-shortening of Shri Sir Ranjitsinhji Vibhaji, famous turn-of-the-century cricketer, who became Maharaja Jam Saheb of Nawanagar. He was educated at Cambridge and played for Sussex and for England against Australia, a most popular and successful batsman. Born 1872: died 1933.

Raw Dealocrat, the: see *the Boss*.

Red Adair: Paul Adair (fl.1960s and 70s), American/Texan oil-well technologist, chiefly famous for putting out fires.

Red Baron, the: Manfred Freiherr von Richthofen (1892–1918), German fighter pilot of the First World War, not only a hero to his own side but greatly respected by Allied airmen. He flew a red Fokker plane and led what became known as **Richthofen's Circus** which created havoc. He was credited with destroying eighty planes. When shot down over Allied lines he was given a military funeral, with a bearer party of six captains and a firing party provided by the Australian Flying Corps.

Red Countess, the: Frances Evelyn Greville, Countess of Warwick (1861–1938) ('Daisy'), one-time mistress of King Edward VII and convert to socialism. Hector Bolitho said: 'Her devotion to the cause of labour was as complete as her early conquests in society.'

Red Dany: see *Danny the Red*.

Red Dean, the: Dr Hewlett Johnson (1874–1965), former Dean of Manchester who became Dean of Canterbury in 1931; often the centre of controversy because of his political views and genuine belief that the Communist ideal was akin to Christian ethics. He travelled widely, including tours of Russia and China, and his last visit to China took place when he was 90.

Red Ken: Ken Livingstone (b.1945), Left-wing leader of the Greater London Council from 1981. His downbeat manner coupled with forthright and at times eccentric policies made him the target of much media attention. See also under 'PRIVATE EYE' NICKNAMES.

Others similarly labelled have been **Red Ted** (Ted Knight), Left-wing leader of Lambeth Council in the early 1980s and **Red Robbo** (Derek Robinson), a trade union 'convener' at British Leyland. In November 1976, when BL was on the brink of collapse he was sacked. Sir Michael Edwardes, the chairman, claimed that his militancy had cost the company £200 million.

Red Robert: Sir Robert Birley (1903−82), headmaster of Charterhouse, Eton, etc. Although somewhat radical for an establishment figure, Birley acquired the nickname by accident. When he was Educational Adviser to the British Military Government in Germany after the war, an English visitor looked in on his office. Birley was not there but the visitor saw a portrait of Karl Marx on the wall. This scandalous piece of information was passed around among Old Etonians. In fact, it was not his office and the portrait was of Brahms not Marx. But the nickname stuck.

Redbreasts: nickname given to the Bow Street runners, special officers attached to Bow Street police court in London who were both writ-servers and detectives. They were disbanded when the Metropolitan Police Force was founded in 1829. They wore a blue coat with brass buttons, usually open and displaying a red waistcoat. They were also called **Robin Redbreasts.**

redcaps: British military police, with red covers on their caps.

redcoats: until the general introduction of khaki, the nickname for British soldiers of the line because of their scarlet tunics, as typically used by Kipling in *Barrack Room Ballads* (1892) − 'The publican 'e up an' sez, "We serve no redcoats here"'. Cromwell introduced the colour for his New Model Army, trimmings in other colours distinguishing the various regiments. In the American War of Independence, George Washington's troops irreverently called the red-coated British **lobsters.** *The Times* correspondent, W. H. Russell, coined the epithet 'the thin red line' when reporting the Crimean War; he was describing the

93rd Highlanders at the Battle of Balaclava, but his words so caught the imagination that they were transferred to British soldiers generally, confronting overwhelming odds with fixed bayonets.

Not to be confused with the name given to male and female attendants at Butlin's holiday camps, so garbed, from the 1950s.

Reds: convenient nickname for Communists since the end of the First World War when it was applied to Bolsheviks, although the colour has been associated with revolutionary movements for much longer, red signifying blood and the spilling of it to gain political ends. It is a gift to newspaper headline writers − 'Reds under the bed', or (*The Observer*, 9 October 1983) 'Reds under the desks', allegations of Marxist indoctrination in the classroom. The international Socialist song, 'The Red Flag', words by Jim Connell, was adopted as a 'signature tune' by the British Labour Party. (Red has not been the only revolutionary colour in England: early in the seventeenth-century Commonwealth it was green, and dissenting soldiers wore green emblems.)

Redshirts: the volunteer force recruited by Giuseppe Garibaldi, also known as 'Garibaldi's thousand', to fight for Italian freedom against Austrians and French. His long and adventurous career was followed sympathetically in Britain, and when in an interval of fighting in 1864 he visited London he was given an enthusiastic reception and the freedom of the city.

Regulars: members of the armed forces who have signed on as a career rather than for a limited period such as a war, the latter called 'for the duration'.

Reluctant Debutante, the: see *the Iron Lady*.

Remittance Men: colonial nickname for immigrants living a usually haphazard kind of life on an allowance sent from home − characters beloved by Victorian and Edwardian fiction writers.

resurrection men: robbers of graves and tombs in order to sell the recently interred bodies to surgical and medical schools for dissection in the latter part of the eighteenth century and the beginning of the next. 'Body snatching', as it was called, was briefly profitable and led to even worse crimes, the most notable being that of William Burke and William Hare who killed people and sold the bodies to an Edinburgh surgeon. Hare turned King's evidence, and Burke was hanged in 1829.

Returned Empties: see *the Fishing Fleet.*

Richard the Lionheart (or **Coeur de Lion**): King Richard I (1157–99) – for his courage though one writer does tell of his plucking out the heart of a lion.

Richthofen's Circus: see *the Red Baron.*

Ringo: Richard Starkey (b.1940), drummer with the Beatles, became known as Ringo Starr (a) because by the age of 20 he was commonly wearing up to four rings (in fact, he was originally called 'Rings') and (b) so his drum solo at Butlin's could be billed as 'Starr Time'.

Robert's Men: see *gentlemen of the road.*

Robin Badfellow: see *the Beaver.*

Robin Redbreasts: see *Redbreasts.*

Romeo, a: originally a young lover, as was Romeo of Juliet in Shakespeare's play, then extended to define a flirtatious 'lady killer'.

Roscius: a talented actor, as was Quintus Roscius Gallus (*c.*126–62 BC) whose graceful manners and diction became proverbial. He excelled in comic parts. Cicero was one of his admirers. Several actors have been compared with him, including David Garrick (1717–79) who was given the honorific, **the English Roscius.** There was also **the Young Roscius,** William Henry West Betty (1791–1874), who first appeared on the stage (in Belfast) at the age of twelve, had great success in Dublin and in Scotland, and appeared at Covent Garden, London, in 1804 when the crowds that gathered to see him were so large that troops had to be called out. On one occasion Pitt adjourned a sitting in the House of Commons so that members could see him at the theatre. He had a few years' fame as a boy actor, retired in 1808, returned to the stage four years later, but the glamour was wearing off. He amassed a large fortune.

Rough Rider: see *the Bull Moose*.

Roundheads: nickname given by the Cavaliers to Parliamentarians and their troops in the Civil War because of their close-cropped hair in contrast with the royalists' longer locks. The term of derision was extended to cover all Cromwell's troops, even though some wore hair to their shoulders. Cromwell himself had fairly long hair.

Royal Martyr, the: see *the Last Man*.

Ruby Nose: see *Nosey*.

Rufus, William: William II (*c*.1056–1100), son of William the Conqueror, so named because of his swarthy or reddish complexion, complementary with his fiery temper. Contemporaries have left an unflattering description of him — fat, sloping shoulders, awkward in gait, suffering from a stutter which made him difficult to understand when excited. Rufus as a nickname has usually been associated with red hair (and there was Barbarossa — red beard — for Frederick I, Holy Roman Emperor, and *le Rougeaud* for Napoleon's Marshal Ney because of his chestnut hair) and a variant of it, russell, has also been a nickname for a fox because of the colour of its fur. (Russell as a surname no doubt comes about in this way.)

Runaway Spartan, the: see *Orange Peel*.

Rupert of Debate, the: 14th Earl of Derby (1799–1869), Conservative Prime Minister, considered to be in the front rank of parliamentary speakers. However, this label was first applied with satirical intent by Disraeli in 1844 when the two men were on opposite sides of the House: 'The noble lord in this case, as in so many others, is the Prince Rupert of parliamentary discussion; his charge is resistless; but when he returns from pursuit he always finds his camp in the possession of the enemy. Also **the Hotspur of Debate.**

S

Sage of Chelsea, the: Thomas Carlyle (1795–1881), historian, essayist and a noted resident of the London borough.

Sage of Monticello, the: Thomas Jefferson (1743–1826), 3rd US President (1801–9). His estate was called Monticello. He was also known as **Long Tom** as he measured 6 feet 3 inches.

Sage of Robertsbridge, the: see *St Mugg*.

Sailor King, the: William IV (1765–1837), a nickname he enjoyed, because he had long wished – as Duke of Clarence, and as a midshipman and then a captain – to have his services to the navy recognised. As duke he fretted about inactivity, not being given a command, and was delighted when – on the death of the Duke of York in 1827 and he became heir to the throne – he was appointed Lord High Admiral. Because of his interference in naval affairs, however, he was asked to resign. See also *Grandpapa England*.

Sailor Prince, the: see *Grandpapa England*.

Saint Mugg: Malcolm Muggeridge (b.1903), writer and broadcaster, who embraced Christianity with particular fervour in his later years. A resident of Robertsbridge, Sussex – hence sometimes known as **the Sage of Robertsbridge.**

Salisbury Plains, the: sisters Lady Maud Cecil (later Selborne) and Lady Gwendolen Cecil, daughters of the 3rd Marquess of Salisbury, unkindly nicknamed thus by Victorian London society because of their unattractive faces.

(Disclosed by Lord David Cecil in his *The Cecils of Hatfield House*, Houghton Mifflin, 1973.)

Sally Lunn: a sweet teacake as made by Sally Lunn, a much-appreciated pastrycook in Bath around 1800. She sold them in the streets herself. They were recommended to be buttered and eaten warm. However, the name may be no more than a corruption of the French *soleil lune*, or sun and moon cake.

Sam Browne: General Sir Samuel James Browne VC (1824–1901) gave his name to the belt he invented, with a strap over the shoulder. It became an essential item of officers' equipment.

Satchmo: Louis Armstrong (1900–71), jazz trumpeter and singer, leader of dance orchestras and world famous for his influence on jazz music and his unique style of improvisation. Armstrong himself said the nickname – a contraction of 'satchel-mouth' – was invented by Percy Mathison Brooks, editor of the *Melody Maker* during his 1932 visit to England. Armstrong had, however, used the word in public and on record before 1932, referring to his trumpet. The name Satchmo has subsequently been given to a type of fungus which exhibits a very large mouth. Armstrong was also called **Pops.**

Scarface Al: (usually shortened to **Scarface**) Al Capone (1899–1947), gangster who terrorised Chicago during the Prohibition era. The scar on his left cheek (usually turned away from cameras) was caused by a razor slash he received in a Brooklyn gang fight in his younger days. According to his biographer, John Kobler, the scar: ' . . . ran along his left cheek from ear to jaw, another across the jaw, and a third below the left ear . . . He was touchy about his disfigurement. He often considered plastic surgery . . . He detested the sobriquet the press had fastened on him . . . and nobody used it in his presence without courting disaster. He allowed his intimates to call him **Snorky** – slang for elegant.'

scarlet woman: a harlot; used as an abusive nickname by early Protestants for the Roman Catholic church, selecting a passage from *Revelation*, 17.

S(c)hnozzle: (or **S(c)hnozzola**) Jimmy Durante (1893–1980), American comedian with a vast nose. A Yiddish word derived from German *schnause* = snout, though Durante was himself Italian Catholic.

Schoolmaster, the: see *the Phrasemaker*.

Scoop: Senator Henry Jackson (1912–83), conservative US Democratic politician. His nickname was derived from a comic strip called 'Scoop, the Cub Reporter' which appeared on page one of the *Everett Daily Herald*, a newspaper which he delivered when a boy in Everett, Wash. His sister, Gertrude, noted the resemblance between her younger brother and the inquisitive reporter.

Scotch-Eggs: see 'PRIVATE EYE' NICKNAMES.

Scotch Wop, the: see BOXERS.

Screen's Master Character Actor, the: see FILM STARS.

Seagreen Incorruptible, the: Maximilien François Marie Isidore de Robespierre (1758–94), French revolutionary leader. He established the Reign of Terror (1793–4) but was executed himself. The name comes from Thomas Carlyle's *History of the French Revolution*. There was no connection between Robespierre's greenness and his incorruptibility. He was green because of his poor digestion, and he was incorruptible because he was a fanatic.

Seducer of the Valleys, the: see GOSSIP COLUMN NICK-NAMES.

Sex Kitten, the: see FILM STARS.

Sex Thimble, the: see FILM STARS.

Sexy Rexy: see FILM STARS.

Sharon: see POP STARS.

Shepherd of the Ocean: Queen Elizabeth's affectionate

nickname for Sir Walter Raleigh (c.1552−1618) in tribute to his sea voyages and colonisation expeditions to America, in fashion with the pastoral poetry of the period. (Her successor, James I, was not so appreciative: Raleigh was accused of plotting against him and was executed.)

Sherpa, the: see 'PRIVATE EYE' NICKNAMES.

She-Wolf, the: see *the Emancipator.*

Shirl the Pearl: see 'PRIVATE EYE' NICKNAMES.

Shit of Persia, the: see 'PRIVATE EYE' NICKNAMES.

Short-thigh: see *Curthose.*

SHOW BUSINESS STARS: Many entertainers use their nicknames as part of their act, so to speak. The labels become like 'bill-matter' or 'strap-lines', those little phrases which describe or promote their acts. Some of the more unusual include:

> **Big Yin, the:** Billy Connolly, Scots comedian. It means 'Big One' and probably derives from a Crucifixion sketch in which he refers to Christ as such.
> **Cheeky Chappie, the:** Max Miller, the comedian who advanced the cause of the *double entendre.*
> **Chocolate Coloured Coon, the:** G. H. Elliott, who blacked up to impersonate a minstrel.
> **Clown Prince of Wales, the:** Wyn Calvin, Welsh comedian. He dropped it in deference to Prince Charles.
> **Darling of the Halls, the:** see *the Prime Minister of Mirth* below.
> **Flip Wilson:** Clerow Wilson, American comedian. When he amused his buddies in the Air Force they apparently thought he had 'flipped out'. Hence the name by which he is now known.
> **Golden Foghorn, the:** Ethel Merman, loud-voiced songstress.
> **Gov'nor, the:** George Edwardes (1852−1915), British the-

atrical manager and impresario, who for nearly thirty years was manager of the Gaiety Theatre, London: he produced many successful musical plays. (Several other 'showbiz' people have been thus named.) And see sep. entry.

Lad 'Imself, the: Tony Hancock, comedian of suburban life.

Last of the Red Hot Mamas, the: Sophie Tucker, singer. From the title of a song by Jack Yellen, introduced by her in 1928.

Little Aussie Bleeder, the: 'Norman Gunston', Australian comic personality, often to be seen with tissue-paper applied to his shaving cuts.

Little Egypt: Stage name of Catherine Devine who made the dance known as the Coochee-Coochee famous from 1893. She had a tendency to dance in the nude.

Little Tich: see sep. entry.

Little Waster, the: Bobby Thompson, Geordie comedian. This was the name his wife used to call him in his variety act (i.e. layabout).

Man With the Golden Trumpet, the: Eddie Calvert.

Man With the Orchid-Lined Voice, the: Enrico Caruso. See sep. entry.

Mr Piano: Joe Henderson, pianist. Always billed as Joe 'Mr Piano' Henderson.

One and Only, the: Phyllis Dixey, strip-tease artist.

Our Gracie: Gracie Fields.

Our Marie: Marie Lloyd. Also **the Queen of the Halls/ Music Hall.**

Pantomime King, the: (1) Julian Wylie (2) Tom Arnold. Both produced lavish pantomimes from the 1930s onwards.

Parrot Face: Freddie Davies, comedian.

Prime Minister of Mirth, the: Sir George Robey (1869– 1954), music hall comedian. This was how he was billed. Also known as **the Darling of the Halls** as a result of an exchange in court. Mr Justice Darling inquired, 'And who is George Robey?' F. E. Smith replied, 'Mr George Robey is the Darling of the music halls, m'lud.'

Prince of Showmen, the: Phineas T. Barnum.

Professor: Jimmy Edwards, comedian, on account of his

Cambridge education and some of the parts (headmasters etc.) he has played.

Ski-nose: Bob Hope.

Stinker: Richard Murdoch, from the days when he appeared in radio's *Band Waggon* with Arthur Askey.

Two-Ton Tessie: Tessie O'Shea, plump songstress (cf. *Two-Ton Tony* in BOXERS). A 22,000-lb RAF bomb in 1945 was accordingly dubbed 'Ten Ton Tessie'.

Velvet Fog, the: see sep. entry.

White-Eyed Kaffir, the: G.H.Chirgwin, another blacked-up minstrel impersonator with distinctive white-diamond eye make-up over one eye.

Wigan Nightingale, the: George Formby Snr, inventor of the 'Wigan Pier' joke — in ironic imitation of *the Swedish Nightingale*.

World's Greatest Entertainer, the: Al Jolson.

See also *Big-hearted Arthur* and POP STARS.

shrieking sisterhood, the: nickname given by their detractors and current between 1908 and 1914 for the Suffragettes, because of their shouted slogans and their sometimes high-pitched harangues at public meetings, especially outdoors.

Shrimp, the: see GOSSIP COLUMN NICKNAMES.

Shylock: a usurer, a merciless moneylender, based on Shylock in *The Merchant of Venice* and probably current as a nickname for nearly 400 years.

Sid Yobbo: see 'PRIVATE EYE' NICKNAMES.

Silent Cal: Calvin Coolidge (1872–1933), 30th US President (1923–9), noted for his taciturnity. When a girl told him of a bet she had placed to get him to say more than three words, he replied, 'You lose.'

Silly Billy: William Frederick, Duke of Gloucester, cousin of William IV to whom the nickname has also been given, but the Duke earned it first. In the wrangles between Whigs and Tories, when the King supported the former, Gloucester is reported to have asked, 'Who is silly Billy now?'

Sinbad the Tailor: Emmanuel (later Lord) Shinwell (b.1884), when he was a rising young trade unionist and efficient agitator at the beginning of the century. The press gave him this ephemeral nickname when, as a representative of the garment workers in Glasgow, he also helped to organise a seamen's strike.

Singer's Singer, the: see *the Velvet Fog*.

Singing Capon, the: see FILM STARS.

Sir Jams: see 'PRIVATE EYE' NICKNAMES.

Sir Reverse: a nickname given in the early part of the Boer War to Sir Redvers Henry Buller (1839–1908), a distinguished soldier who had won the VC in the Zulu War but when in command of the campaign in South Africa he was no match for the Boers, and his army suffered reverses at Colenso and Spion Kop. He was replaced by Lord Roberts, nicknamed *Bobs*.

Sir Sheath: see 'PRIVATE EYE' NICKNAMES.

Sir Shortly Floorcross: Sir Hartley Shawcross (b.1902), later Lord Shawcross. A former Labour politician who changed his allegiance ('crossed the floor', as in the House of Commons).

Sir Veto: (1) Andrew Johnson (1808–75), 17th US President (1865–69). A conservative on race relations he twice used his veto to prohibit liberal legislation but Congress managed to ignore this. In all he used his veto twenty-one times during his Presidency. Also: **His Accidency** – he succeeded Lincoln after the assassination.

(2) Grover Cleveland. See *the Man of Destiny*.

Ski-nose: see SHOW BUSINESS STARS.

skyjacker: a person who takes over an aircraft in flight, forcing the pilot to do his bidding; created in the 1970s when this type of hijacking became prevalent.

sky pilot: armed forces' nickname for a padre in the First World War, rarely used in the Second.

Slapsie Maxie: see BOXERS.

Slicker of Wakefield, the: see 'PRIVATE EYE' NICKNAMES.

Sligger: Francis F. Urquhart (−1935), noted Oxford don.

Sloane Ranger: the term (echoing a Western character, The Lone Ranger) was coined by Peter York in 1975 and cultivated in the magazine *Harpers and Queen* to describe a type of posh, country girl of good family, on the look-out for a husband. She lives in a flat around Sloane Square in London, probably sharing, and has an artistic job, does social service work, or teaches in a nursery school. When the Princess of Wales (**Supersloane**) entered public life the phenomenon became much more generally understood and was the subject of books by York with Ann Barr, though these broadened the term to include other areas of British upper middle class existence.

York has also found names for **Foodies**, people who take an inordinate amount of interest in the pursuit or preparation of good food, **Mayfair Mercs** (flashy, mercenary gold-diggers, perhaps driving a Mercedes, who look as if they have already dug it), and **Noovos** (or **Noovs**), a new name for the old *nouveaux riches* whose 'spiritual home is a lift in a smart department store'.

Smith of Smiths, the: Macaulay's nickname for the witty writer and clergyman Sydney Smith (1771−1845), a founder and first editor of *The Edinburgh Review* who became a distinguished preacher and lecturer in London and a canon of St Paul's.

Smokey/ Smokin' Joe: see BOXERS.

Smoothiechops: see 'PRIVATE EYE' NICKNAMES.

Smuggins: Nigel Lawson (b.1932), Conservative politician. So dubbed by his schoolmates at Westminster.

Snapshots/ Snowbum/ Snowdrop: see GOSSIP COLUMN NICKNAMES.

Snobby Roberts: see *the Iron Lady*.

Snorky: see *Scarface Al*.

Soapy Sam: Samuel Wilberforce (1805–73), Bishop of Oxford, later of Winchester, powerful preacher and persuasive in argument, while at the same time trying to smooth things over between men of opposing points of view. (He opposed Huxley, however, when the latter defended Darwin's evolutionary theories.) He was noted for his wit, and his own explanation of the nickname was that he often got into hot water but emerged with clean hands. Others considered him to be unctuous.

sob sister: like an **agony aunt**, a journalist who answers readers' questions dealing with intimate problems, allowing the writers to weep on her shoulders. Although the term may be of American invention such an adviser has long been known in British ladies' magazines, the subjects formerly being mainly in household management, etiquette and bringing up a family. Such columnists proliferated after the Second World War and some achieved eminence for their expert and sympathetic advice and information.

Sooty: see GOSSIP COLUMN NICKNAMES.

Spam: see GOSSIP COLUMN NICKNAMES.

spencer: a short overcoat or jacket, as supplied to the 2nd Earl Spencer (1785–1834). Several items have been named 'spencer', including a man's wig and a woman's bodice.

Sphinx: see *the Boss*.

spiv: one who lives on his wits, making money without really working, usually nattily dressed as he goes about his business: 'a relentless opportunist, a picker-up of considerable as well as unconsidered trifles', as Eric Partridge defines him in *Here There and Everywhere*, 1950. The origin of the word is obscure: late in the nineteenth century it was used for a bookmaker's runner; during the earlier part of the twentieth it was identified with a smart and non-violent operator on the fringe of actual crime, coming into his own in wartime and post-war rationing 'black markets'.

Sprat: see *Grandpapa England*.

squarson: combination of 'squire' and 'parson', as were so many incumbents in eighteenth- and nineteenth-century England.

Squire of Hyde Park, the: see *the Boss*.

Stage-door Johnnies: men-about-town, wealthy and often aristocratic who waited at the stage doors of London theatres in late Victorian and Edwardian times for their favourite dancers and actresses, the nickname current roughly between the 1870s and 1914. They were especially identified with the Gaiety Theatre and Daly's, particularly the former whose famous Gaiety Girls often 'married well', some into the peerage.

Stalin's Granny: Joan Maynard (b.1921), charming Left-wing British MP.

Steelboys: see *the Babes in the Wood*.

Steel Magnolia, the: Rosalynn Carter (b.1927), wife of President Jimmy Carter. The First Lady's role apparently went further than holding hands with her husband in public. He consulted her on policy matters and she seems to have had some influence over his decisions. The magnolia is a flower particularly associated with southern US areas.

Steenie: George Villiers, 1st Duke of Buckingham (1592–1628), favourite of James I who gave him high honours and this nickname, alluding to Stephen (*Acts*,6) who was 'full of grace' and people 'saw that his face was like the face of an angel'. Villiers's youthful charm delighted the king, but as his power and influence grew — he was for a time virtually ruler of England — he undertook more than he could accomplish in foreign affairs. Parliament attacked him, and a man with a grievance stabbed him to death.

Stepfather of His Country, the: see *the Father of His Country*.

Stevarse: see 'PRIVATE EYE' NICKNAMES.

Stewpot: see DISC JOCKEYS.

Sticks: see *Twiggy*.

Stills: see *Bennies*.

Sting: see POP STARS.

Stinker: see SHOW BUSINESS STARS.

Stockport 6, the: see *the Chicago 7*.

Stonewall: Thomas J. Jackson (1824–63), Confederate general in the American Civil War. He won this nickname at the First Battle of Bull Run, 21 July 1861. One Barnard Bee is said to have remarked, 'See, there is Jackson, standing like a stone-wall.' The verb 'to stonewall', meaning to obstruct, may derive from this idea of steadfastness, and it has long been used in cricket for cautious batsmanship.

strad: contraction of Antonio Stradivari (*c.*1644–1737) used as nickname for a violin made by him — perhaps the greatest craftsman in this field — or in his workshop in the Italian city of Cremona, a centre for this particular skill. 'Cremona' is another nickname for a violin made by him or by the Amati brothers and Guarnieri.

street arabs: Victorian name for poor boys, wandering (like Arabs) in the streets. They earned a few pennies by sweeping street crossings: they begged, and their wanderings led them into petty crime.

Strongbow: Richard de Clare, 2nd Earl of Pembroke, who succeeded to his father's estates in 1148, did much fighting in Ireland and was beloved by his soldiers who gave him this nickname. He was tall and fair, courteous and wise, as well as being a man of valour.

Stuffed Prophet, the: see *the Man of Destiny*.

Stupenda, La: Joan Sutherland (b.1926), Australian opera singer of impressive mien. Also **the Glorious Iceberg.**

submerged tenth: the poorer, unnoticed people, an appellation given by William Booth, founder of the Salvation Army, to destitutes and unemployables.

Suffragettes: the most respectable (and abiding) nickname given to the women who campaigned early in the century for permission to vote: others, like *the shrieking sisterhood*, were vituperative. Mrs Emmeline Pankhurst and her husband founded the Women's Franchise League in 1889, and in 1903 formed the Women's Social and Political Union. She and her daughters, Christabel and Sylvia, were tireless organisers and public speakers. The suffragette movement as a militant force began at the Free Trade Hall, Manchester in 1905 − as a plaque in the hall commemorates − when Christabel and Annie Kenney were thrown out of a meeting, continued their protest in the street, were arrested and sent to prison. Meetings, petitions, demonstrations − and occasional violence − eventually won the vote for women.

Sugar Ray Robinson: see BOXERS.

Sultan of Swat, the: see *the Babe*.

Sundance Kid, the: see *Butch*.

Sun King, the: (le Roi Soleil) Louis XIV (1638−1715), King of France (1643−1715). It was fitting that the part in a masque for which he was sumptuously dressed at the age of fifteen − 'The Sun King' − and of which there was a popular engraving, should be retained as a title because of his brilliant court.

Sunny Jim: James Callaghan (b.1912), Labour politician and Prime Minister (1976–79). He had a ready, bank-manager smile in the face of adversity, though the nonchalant inquiry 'Crisis? What crisis?' pinned on him during the industrial troubles of 1979's 'Winter of Discontent' may have cost him the subsequent election. (The original 'Sunny Jim' was a cartoon character advertising Force breakfast cereal from *c.*1903.)

Superbrat: John McEnroe (b.1959) American tennis player and men's Champion at Wimbledon. Notorious for his spoilt child behaviour on court, arguing with umpires, linesmen, crowds, anybody. Also **Mac the Mouth.**

Supermac: Harold Macmillan (b.1894), Conservative Prime Minister (1957–63), later Earl of Stockton. The nickname was created by the political cartoonist Vicky in a drawing for the *Evening Standard* (6 November 1958) showing Macmillan dressed as Superman. Like Aneurin Bevan's coinage **Macwonder,** this nickname was originally ironic in intent but came to lose that overtone in the early part of Macmillan's premiership when he exerted a great flair for relaxed showmanship. In 1962 he became known as **Mac the Knife** when he sacked seven cabinet ministers (including the Chancellor of the Exchequer) in a 'night of the long knives' exercise.

Supersloane: see *Sloane Ranger*.

Svengali: see *trilby*.

Swan of Avon, the: see *the Bard of Avon*.

Swan of Lichfield, the: Anna Seward (1747–1809), poet and author, admired and visited by Dr Johnson in his home town of Lichfield where she lived. She in return admired him to adulation. Later Sir Walter Scott edited her poetical works.

Swan of Pesaro, the: Gioacchino Antonio Rossini (1792–1868), the composer, especially of opera including the *Barber of Seville* and *William Tell*. He was born at Pesaro, the resort in eastern Italy.

Sweater Girl, the: see FILM STARS.

Swedish Nightingale, the: Jenny (Johanna Maria) Lind (1820–87), whose great talents as a singer made her famous in Europe (especially Germany and Britain) and in America. She excelled in opera and Handel's *Messiah*. England was her home in the latter part of her life, and she died at Malvern. In the USA, her nickname gave rise to the term 'Irish Nightingale' for a bullfrog.

Sweet Nell: see *Nell of Old Drury*.

Sweet Swan of Avon: see *the Bard of Avon*.

T

Tail-end Charlie: the rear gunner in a bomber; also the last in a flight of aircraft.

talking heads: broadcasting nickname for the type of TV programme which is composed mainly of people talking, shown in 'head and shoulder' shots and/or addressing the camera directly. Often used critically by those who would prefer a programme to show more physical action or to get out and about away from the studio.

tallyman: salesman (hawker and shopkeeper) providing goods on credit, payment by instalments being recorded – originally by notches on a stick (from the French *taille*, notch), going back to the fifteenth century. Hence 'tally shop' and the verb to 'tally', meaning to correspond with, or duplicate – salesman and customer checking their notches.

tantalus: a stand of decanters, visible but in a locked frame, commemorating Tantalus, son of Zeus in Greek mythology, who was condemned to stand in Hell with water and fruit just out of reach – tantalising! The nickname with domestic servants in mind became a dictionary word.

Tante Yvonne: Mme Yvonne de Gaulle (d.1979) wife of President Charles de Gaulle. The name 'Aunt Yvonne' came from her homely nature. On the day of one of the assassination attempts against her husband, she had bought two chickens in aspic. She took them with her when she accompanied the President in his car. Her first question on finding out that her husband was all right was to ask if anything had happened to the chickens.
(Cf. *Yvonne* in 'PRIVATE EYE' NICKNAMES)

tantivy: derisory nickname for high churchmen at the time of James II's support for Roman Catholics, based on a caricature of such clergymen mounted on the church of Rome and 'riding tantivy' (that is, at a gallop) to Rome.

Tarzan: see 'PRIVATE EYE' NICKNAMES.

Teapot: see GOSSIP COLUMN NICKNAMES.

Teddy: nowadays the inevitable shortening of any man called Edward or Theodore. One of the most notable bearers of the nickname was Theodore Roosevelt, the US President (see *the Bull Moose*). The 'teddy bear' was named directly after him because of an incident in 1903 — the second year of his presidency — when on a bear shoot in Mississippi. His hosts stunned a small brown bear and tied it to a tree so that he would be sure to make a kill. After this, manufacturers of stuffed toy bears renamed their product. See also *Tum-Tum*.

Teddy Boys: youths who adopted Edwardian style of dress in the 1950s and behaved bullyingly and violently, clashing with the public and police; elegant in appearance, antisocial in outlook; smarter precursors of 'hell's angels' who took to leather jackets and motor-bikes, and 'mods' and 'rockers'.

Terriers: members of the British Territorial Army, formed in 1907, now reconstituted and given the title (since 1967) of the Territorial and Army Volunteer Reserve.

Thatch: see CRICKETERS.

That (Mad) Man in the White House: see *the Boss*.

Thief of Badgags, the: see *Mr Television*.

Thinking Man's Crumpet, the: Joan Bakewell (b.1933), TV presenter — most notably on BBC2's *Late Night Line-up* in the 1960s — with intelligence and faintly *blue stocking* good looks. So dubbed by Frank Muir, no doubt to the lady's annoyance.

Threat, the: see FILM STARS.

Thunderer, the: Edward Sterling (1773–1847) who, under the pseudonym of Vetus, wrote vigorous letters to *The Times* which were reprinted, and in 1815 he joined the staff and became virtual editor under Thomas Barnes, continuing his robust and crusading style, with such expressions as 'We thundered forth the other day . . . ' The nickname conferred on him was quickly transferred to the paper itself, so that *The Times* became 'The Thunderer'.

Thunder-thighs: see GOSSIP COLUMN NICKNAMES.

Tich: see *Little Tich*.

Tiger, the: Georges Clemenceau (1841–1929), French statesman who was given the title when he toppled one ministry after another from 1876. As a member of the Chamber and as Prime Minister he instituted many reforms, and the nickname clung to him with especial significance for his inflexible attitude in the First World War.

Tin Lizzie: hardly a 'personality' but humanised enough by the owners of Henry Ford's Model T motor-car, the first mass-produced vehicle, inelegant but efficient and comparatively cheap. Fifteen million were produced between 1908 and discontinuation of the model in 1927. Mr Ford is said to have encouraged jokes about them for the sake of publicity as they rattled around the world. 'Lizzie' may be a contraction of 'limousine'.

Tina: see *the Iron Lady*.

Tiny Rowland: see GOSSIP COLUMN NICKNAMES.

Tip: Thomas P. O'Neill Jr (b.1912), US Democratic Congressman, Speaker of the House of Representatives.

Tippecanoe: (or **Old Tippecanoe**) William Henry Harrison

(1773—1841), 9th US President (1841). He had defeated Indians at Tippecanoe Creek in 1811 and was also known as **the Log Cabin Candidate** because he came from the west of the USA where log cabins were still the thing.

Titian-Haired Temptress, the: see 'PRIVATE EYE' NICK-NAMES.

toad-eater: assistant to a *quack* doctor, usually a boy, who ate a toad (believed to be poisonous) — or pretended to do so — at the command of his master who promptly 'cured' him to impress the crowds on village green or fairground. Changed to 'toady', the nickname came to indicate an obsequious person, one who will do anything to please.

Toadthrush: see 'PRIVATE EYE' NICKNAMES.

Tokyo Rose: name given by US servicemen to Iva Ikuko Toguri D'Aquino (b.1916), whose voice broadcasting to them on Japanese radio in the Second World War told them they were sacrificing home comforts in a futile fight against invincible forces.

Tolpuddle Martyrs, the: six farm labourers from the Dorset-shire village of Tolpuddle who formed a union to improve their conditions and were sentenced to transportation to Australia in 1834 on a charge of administering illegal oaths. The government at that time was concerned about working-class unrest. There was a public outcry and demonstrations on the Tolpuddle men's behalf, and they were pardoned two years later.

Tom, Dick and Harry: every ordinary man (these being common names); a Victorian expression which has per-sisted for 'man-in-the-street'.

tom-fool: an idiotic kind of fellow, often up to pranks, at least as old as the sixteenth century, one of several nick-names incorporating Tom, the diminutive of Thomas which has always been a common Christian name: cf. 'tom-noddy', a feckless person or a blockhead, and 'tom-cat', a male of the feline species.

Tommy (Atkins): the British 'other ranks' soldier, from the specimen signature of Thomas Atkins on attestation forms and other documents. The Duke of Wellington may have been instrumental in finding the name. According to Elizabeth Longford, *Wellington: Pillar of State* (Weidenfeld & Nicolson, 1972), in 1815, in the first weeks after Waterloo: 'A military paper had been submitted to him suggesting a typical name for a private. The Duke crossed out the entry and substituted the name of a veteran in his old regiment, the 33rd Foot. Private Thomas Atkins had been with him during the engagement at Boxtel in 1794.'

'Tommy' spread throughout the empire and the world as the nickname for the ordinary British soldier:

> O it's Tommy this, an' Tommy that, an' 'Tommy, go away';
> But it's 'Thank you, Mister Atkins', when the band begins to play.'

Kipling, *Barrack Room Ballads*, 1892.

Tom o' Bedlam: a beggar, pleading insanity.

Tom Thumb: Charles Sherwood Stratton (1838–83), an American dwarf who was dubbed 'General' Tom Thumb when he toured with P. T. Barnum's show. He was about 2 feet high when first exhibited, but he grew to about 3 feet 4 inches, and in 1863 he married another dwarf called Lavinia. He and his wife were received by President Lincoln, and by Queen Victoria when they came to England. The nickname came from very old fairy tales, the hero being the size of a giant's thumb.

Tories: abusive nickname for Irish Roman Catholics, and formerly for dispossessed Irish of the sixteenth and seventeenth centuries who became outlaws and attacked English settlers and soldiers, from an Irish word meaning 'pursuit'. The nickname was transferred to those Englishmen who opposed the exclusion of the Duke of York from the throne as James II (he was a Roman Catholic), and hence to the political party that was formed in the Cavalier tradition. Towards the end of the seventeenth century the opposing political ideologies lined up as Whigs and Tories, the supporters of each flinging nicknames at each other, because *Whigs* is also a nickname. It is yet another example of a sneering nickname being absorbed as a respectable word, although 'Whigs' has faded from use whereas 'Tories' is retained as a convenient alternative to the 'Conservative' party which took its title under Peel and Disraeli.

Tragedy Queen of the British Stage, the: see *Black Jack*.

travellers (or **travelling people**): gypsies.

Tricky Dick: Richard Milhous Nixon (b.1913), US President (1969–74), who resigned after the 'Watergate' scandal. So dubbed at the start of his career by Helen Gahagan Douglas in 1950. During an election campaign in California he had hinted that she was a fellow-traveller. Despite his many later achievements, the nickname was generally adopted to indicate Nixon's art of political manipulation and evasion. Also **the Bela Lugosi of American Politics** (for his grim appearance, reminiscent of the horror film star) and **the Houdini of American Politics** (for his early agility in getting out of scrapes).

trilby: soft felt hat with crown indented, as worn by Beerbohm Tree in the play (from the novel) of that name by George du Maurier. Tree took the part of Svengali, the sinister influence on the artist's model, Trilby. His stage hat at the turn of the century was floppier than the present 'trilby' but it set a fashion. **Svengali** became the (somewhat sinister) nickname for any behind-the-scenes figure thought to have masterminded the success of a public personality.

Trimmer, the: George Savile, 1st Marquess of Halifax (1633–95), eloquent and able statesman whose complete detachment from either Whigs or Tories antagonised both parties. Embroiled in all the great issues of the day he advocated compromise, trimming his sails to suit the political winds, and admitted his nickname even to the extent of writing a pamphlet entitled *The Character of a Trimmer*.

Tubby: Revd P. B. Clayton (1885–1972), founder of Toc H (Talbot House) during the First World War. This was a church institute opened at Poperinghe, Belgium, in 1915 for soldiers in the Ypres salient and was named after an officer who was killed – G. W. L. Talbot, son of a Bishop of Winchester.

Tumbledown Dick: see *Queen Dick*.

Tum-Tum: Edward VII (1841–1910), King of Great Britain and Ireland (1901–10). Most of his nicknames refer either to his amorous activities or, like this one, to his upholstery. His mother, Queen Victoria, called him **Bertie** (one of his Christian names was Albert, after his father). He was accorded the honorific **Edward the Peacemaker** for his part in cementing the Entente Cordiale with France and was known as **the Uncle of Europe** because the German Kaiser was his nephew, and the Queens of Spain and Norway and the Tsarina of Russia were his nieces. Through his wife Alexandra he was also uncle to the Kings of Greece and Denmark and the ill-fated Nicholas II, Tsar of Russia. He inherited the nickname from his mother, Queen Victoria, known as *the Grandmother of Europe*. For his amorous activities, he was known variously as **Teddy**, **Old Peacock**, and – jokingly – as **Edward the Caresser** or, later, as 'Edward the Piecemaker' (and the piece he made was Lily Langtry . . .)

Turnip-hoer, the: George I (1660–1727) who was said to have suggested turning St James's Park in London into a turnip field.

Twiggy: nickname that became the professional name of Lesley Hornby (b.1946), 'Cos my legs are all peculiar and thin like twigs, see.' This slim London girl whose distinctive looks and personality brought her fame as a model in the 1960s later went on to a stage and film career as singer and dancer. Her nickname at school was **Sticks.**

twitchers: amateur ornithologists. Bird-watchers 'twitch' with excitement at the sight of a rare species.

Two-Dinners: see 'PRIVATE EYE' NICKNAMES.

Two-Ton Tessie: see SHOW BUSINESS STARS.

Two-Ton Tony: see BOXERS.

Tycoon, the: see *the Emancipator*.

U

uncle: a pawnbroker, in use since the mid-eighteenth century, probably to liken him to a helpful relative.

Uncle Joe: see *Man of Steel*.

Uncle Miltie: see *Mr Television*.

Uncle of Europe, the: see *Tum-Tum*.

Uncle Paul: (Oom Paul in Afrikaans) Paul (Paulus) Kruger (1825–1904), four times elected President of the Transvaal republic, an 'uncle' if not 'father' figure in his own domain and in South Africa generally, although his political career was controversial. His aim was the domination of South Africa by the Boers, and the nickname was current during the Boer (or South African) War.

Uncle Sam: personification of the USA as *John Bull* is of England. The name has been used since early in the nineteenth century, most likely an invention based on the initials US on government supplies to the forces (as with *GIs*).

Unconditional Surrender: see *the Butcher*.

Uncrowned King of Ireland, the: Charles Stewart Parnell (1846–91), Irish politician, leader of the Irish party in the House of Commons and a valiant fighter for Home Rule. His extremely active and distinguished career was blighted when he was cited as co-respondent in a divorce case: he married the lady, Mrs O'Shea, in 1891.

Uninvited Guest, the: see 'PRIVATE EYE' NICKNAMES.

Unready, the: see *Ethelred the Unready*.

Unwashed: see *the Great Unwashed*.

Upper Ten: short for upper ten thousand, American high society, thought to have been coined by the author and journalist Nathaniel Parker Willis (1806−67), at first describing the élite of New York.

Ursa Major: see *Dictionary Johnson*.

Usurer of the Valleys, the: see 'PRIVATE EYE' NICKNAMES.

V

Valley Girl: American pubescent teenage girl (aged 13 to 17) of a type first observed and identified in California's San Fernando Valley in the early 1980s. She is from a fairly well-to-do family, her passions are shopping, junk food, cosmetics, and speaking in a curious language — 'fer shurr', 'totally', 'gag me with a spoon', 'grody to the max'.

vamp: a flirtatious and predatory woman, a jocular shortening of 'Vampire' and much in vogue in the early silent film days. Frederic Thrasher in *Okay for Sound* (New York, 1946) comments: 'The innocent heroine of the serial was soon supplanted in public favour by the "Vamp", and the film gained in sophistication what it lost in simple morality. Billed as the "wickedest face in the world", Theda Bara not only symbolized this new siren, she played her to the hilt.'

vandyke: a collar or cape slit into points, usually bordered by lace, as worn in portraits by Sir Anthony Van Dyck (1599–1641), Flemish artist at the court of Charles I. The anglicised version of his name also became the nickname for a neatly pointed beard, which was also called a **Charlie** after the royal sitter himself, the king wearing a beard of that fashion.

Velveteens: mid-Victorian nickname for a gamekeeper, because so many on the large estates wore jackets (and perhaps trousers) of this fabric, closely woven cotton with a velvet pile; also an appropriate name because the furry covering over the growing antlers of a deer is called velvet.

Velvet Fog, the: Mel Tormé (b.1923), American singer noted for his smooth crooning style. In 1983, he commented: 'By the age of 18 I'd been labelled **the Singer's Singer** and, although I agree it's a lovely label, I'm anti-labels . . . I was known as The Velvet Fog. I was a little churlish about it at first but later I realised it was an affectionate thing.'

Vicar of Hell, the: two people carried this nickname in the reign of Henry VIII – John Skelton, who had been tutor to Henry when he was a young prince and became rector of Diss in Norfolk, and Poet Laureate; and Sir Francis Bryan, a favourite at court who took the news of Anne Boleyn's condemnation to Jane Seymour, Henry's future wife. Bryan had some hand in his cousin Anne's downfall. King Henry playfully gave Skelton the nickname, punning on the word Diss, an old alternative for Pluto, god of the lower regions, and Skelton's satirical verses and the scandals credited to him strengthened the reference. Thomas Cromwell, Chamberlain to Henry, is said to have given Bryan his nickname.

Vicar of Mirth, the: see SHOW BUSINESS STARS.

Viennese Teardrop, the: see FILM STARS.

Vinegar Joe: General Joseph Stilwell (1883–1946) – because of the 'acidity with which he expressed his opinions'. During the Second World War, he was recalled from his command of Chinese and American troops in China-Burma-India after his tongue-lashing caused trouble with Chiang Kai-Shek in 1944. Also known as **Old Turkey Neck** because of his unusually sunburned face and neck when in Burma.

Violet Corporal, the: see *Boney*.

Virgin Queen, the: see *Gloriana*.

Voice, the: see *Gov'nor*.

W

wallflowers: girls on the edge of the dance floor hoping for partners, backs to the wall like modest country flowers growing against the stonework.

Waltz King, the: Johann Strauss (1825—99), Austrian composer, especially of the Blue Danube Waltz (1867).

Warming Pan baby, the: see *the Old Pretender*.

Warrior Queen, the: Boadicea (died AD 62), queen of the Iceni, who led a revolt against Roman rule in Britain.

Wedgie: Anthony Wedgwood ('Tony') Benn (b.1925), Labour politician. When he was Secretary of State for Industry during the government of 1974—9, he was called 'Wedgie' not only as a contraction of his name but because his Conservative opponents saw him driving a wedge of complete socialism into the constitution, with his plans for nationalisation and seeming hostility towards private enterprise. As a result of his **Bennery**, for a while he became the Left-wing bogeyman of British politics and a music hall joke.
(Incidentally, his pet-name to family and friends is 'Jimmy'.)

Weepers: hired mourners at a funeral, men in black suits and top hats, standing at the door of the house of bereavement and gravely accompanying the cortege, a nineteenth-century custom for those who could afford these dismal gentry. The nickname was also applied to the black veils worn by women and the black bands on the men's hats. (It was also a nickname for long side whiskers, usually called 'Piccadilly Weepers', as worn by fashionable young men for a short period during the century.)

wellingtons: originally a high boot reaching to the knee and cut away behind, as worn on horseback by the 1st Duke of Wellington when on campaign, the name persisting for the high rubber boot which superseded leather.

Welsh Wizard, the: (1) David Lloyd George, Earl of Dwyfor, (1863–1945), because of his long and eventful political career, his oratory and his skill in debate. Among his many offices were those of Chancellor and Prime Minister, and he was a driving force throughout the First World War and a powerful influence at the Peace Conference which followed. Although born in Manchester he was brought up in Wales and represented a Welsh constituency in the House of Commons.

(2) Billy Meredith, footballer, who captained the Manchester City team in the Cup Final of 1904.

(3) Neil Kinnock (b.1942), Leader of the Labour Party since 1983. Partly an inevitable name for a politician obvious for his Welshness, partly mocking. His garrulous manner has also earned him the nickname **the Welsh Windbag.**

Wets: originally 'wet' was a prep school term meaning feeble or timid but in the summer of 1979 it began to take on a new emphasis. It may not actually have come from the lips of Prime Minister Margaret Thatcher herself but the word was applied to those in her Cabinet and party who were opposed to the hard-line monetarist theories then being espoused. However, any pejorative sting was eroded by the enthusiasm with which some of the Wets embraced the name. Those who were less deviant were known as **Dries.**

Whennies: see *Bennies.*

Whigs: the tit-for-tat nickname given by their opponents (*Tories*) to the party which argued for parliamentary power over the crown and advocated toleration for dissenters at the Restoration. The court party — the Tories — was nicknamed after Irish outlaws, and the Whigs got their abusive name from Scottish rebels and horse-thieves, 'whig' probably coming from *whigamore*. There have been other ingenious attempts at the derivation of the word, one of them being that it comprised the initials of the Covenanters' motto 'We hope in God', and certainly it was once applied to them. Whatever the explanation, Whigs and Tories were lined up against each other from the latter part of the seventeenth century, although their policies changed over the years, and Whigs became dominant in the following century. Whigs lost their name to 'Liberals', but the Tories kept theirs as an alternative to 'Conservatives'. Why this should be so is difficult to explain. The nickname was used in the USA for the party which opposed President Andrew Jackson.

Whip: a member of a parliamentary party chosen to ensure the attendance of his colleagues at important debates in the chamber, especially necessary when a government has a small majority and every vote is needed at a division; the word taken from the Whip, the man responsible for the hounds in a hunt. Whips also arrange 'pairing' with an opposition party when members have to be absent at voting time in the House of Commons.

Whiplash/ Whipper Wallace: see GOSSIP COLUMN NICKNAMES.

whipping boy: a person who takes the blame; also transferred to someone held responsible for misdemeanours. The term, or nickname, originated in the boy employed in a royal household to receive such punishment on behalf of the young prince who had merited it from his tutor.

Whispering Grass: Shaw Taylor (b.1924), presenter of ITV's *Police Five* programmes since the 1960s. Asking the public to come forward with information to help solve crimes, Taylor attracted this name in the underworld. 'Whispering Grass' is the title of a popular song and 'grass' is underworld slang for an informer.

White-Eyed Kaffir: see SHOW BUSINESS STARS.

White Queen, the: Mary, Queen of Scots (1542−87) who wore the continental traditional white while in mourning for her first husband, Francis II of France, whereas black was more customary in Scotland and England.

Wickedest Man in the World, the: see *the Beast 666*.

Widow at Windsor, the: Queen Victoria (1819–1901), apt nickname popularised in verse by Rudyard Kipling because she withdrew from public life after the death of Albert, the Prince Consort, living quietly at Windsor Castle. It is said she was displeased with such verses as:

> Then 'ere's to the Widow at Windsor,
>   An' 'ere's to the stores and the guns,
> The men an' the 'orses what makes up the forces
>   O' Missis Victorier's sons.

She was also known as **the Grandmother of Europe** because of her wide circle of relations in European monarchies.

Wigan Nightingale, the: see SHOW BUSINESS STARS.

Wild Bill: (1) James Butler Hickock (1837–76), US frontiersman and marshal. The nickname probably arose during his wilder days when – in 1861 – he challenged a whole crowd to a fight. All the people scattered.

(2) William J. Donovan (1883–1959), US lawyer and statesman, founder of the Office of Strategic Services, the first spy agency in the USA.

Wild Bull of the Pampas, the: see BOXERS.

William the Conqueror: see Preface.

William the Silent: William I (1533–84), Prince of Orange and Count of Nassau, who was given this title (*le Taciturne*) when a young man at the French court because of his discretion, and it stuck to him throughout his turbulent life. He was certainly not untalkative. He was a brave and eloquent leader of resistance against Spanish domination of the

Netherlands, and deeply religious. He was assassinated as he was leaving his dining hall at Delft.

Wilmington 10, the: see *the Chicago 7*.

Winchester Geese: prostitutes living in houses in the Southwark district of London owned by the Bishop of Winchester. Property in this area began to be turned into brothels from the fourteenth century, and by Shakespeare's time was familiar to his audiences. 'Winchester goose!' cries the Duke of Gloucester to the Bishop of Winchester in *1 King Henry the Sixth*, I:ii: ' . . . out, scarlet hypocrite!'

Windsor Cassel: Sir Ernest Cassel (1852−1921), financier and close friend of Edward VII (whom, incidentally, he greatly resembled).

Winkle: see 'PRIVATE EYE' NICKNAMES.

Winnie: Sir Winston Churchill (1874−1965) whose long, adventurous and brilliant career as statesman and writer reached its zenith when he was the inspiring Prime Minister during the Second World War. The nickname had an affectionate ring about it. He himself clung to the code-name **Former Naval Person** in his wartime cables to President Roosevelt (he had been referred to as 'Naval Person' when First Lord of the Admiralty at the outbreak of war).

Wisest Fool in Christendom, the: see *the British Solomon*.

Wislon: see 'PRIVATE EYE' NICKNAMES.

Wizard of Kinderhook, the: see *Little Magician*.

Wizard of the North, the: see *the Great Unknown*.

Wobbling Willie: William (later Lord) Whitelaw (b.1918), Conservative politician whose offices included Home Secretary and Deputy Prime Minister. This nickname was current in 1983 when he had to fend-off embarrassing political questions from the Labour Party. See also 'PRIVATE EYE' NICKNAMES.

Woodbine Willie: Revd Geoffrey Studdert Kennedy MC (d.1929), poet and chaplain in the First World War — renowned for his courage and humility. Troops gave him this nickname because of his habit of walking through the trenches or casualty stations with a haversack full of Woodbine cigarettes. He chatted with the soldiers and always had some 'fags' to offer the men in his care. As an ordained minister he was enrolled as a Forces' chaplain in 1916 and served until 1919.

Woolton Pie: a combination of carrots, parsnips, turnips and potatoes, covered with white sauce and pastry, named after Frederick Marquis, 1st Earl Woolton (1883–1964), Minister of Food 1940–3. Generally admired, Woolton encouraged cooks to make use of whatever foodstuffs were available in wartime but the unappreciated 'Woolton Pie' was his one failure.

World's Greatest Actress, the: see FILM STARS.

World's Greatest Entertainer, the: see SHOW BUSINESS STARS.

World's Most Prolific Novelist, the: see *the Animated Meringue*.

World's Sweetheart, the: see FILM STARS.

Worzel Gummidge: see 'PRIVATE EYE' NICKNAMES.

Woy: see 'PRIVATE EYE' NICKNAMES.

Y

yankee: originally applied to a citizen of New England, then to one residing in the northern states generally, although the British have used the nickname without much geographical reference — in the First World War to any American soldier — 'the Yanks are here'. There are several suggested origins. One is that it was how some North American Indians pronounced 'English' or the way they heard French settlers use the word *Anglais*. Another idea — and perhaps a more likely one — is that early seventeenth-century Dutch settlers in New Amsterdam (the present city of New York) applied the nickname 'Jankin', a diminutive of Jan (John), to the English of Connecticut, and the word became corrupted to 'yankee'. British soldiers in the American War of Independence classed all their opponents as 'yankees', and in the Civil War the confederates used the word for the union (northern) soldiers. 'Yankee Doodle' was an American song popular in England.

Yankee Nigger, the: see BOXERS.

Yankee Sullivan: see BOXERS.

Yardbird: see JAZZ MUSICIANS.

Yes-man: one who for diplomatic or sycophantic reasons always agrees with his superior, reluctant or unable to say 'No'.

Yorkshire Ripper, the: Peter Sutcliffe (b.1946), who murdered some thirteen women in the period 1975—80. The name was first applied by a Yorkshire newspaper during the course of a prolonged police pursuit.

Young Chevalier, the: see *the Young Pretender*.

Young Fogey: a man below the age of 40 who dresses and behaves as if he were prematurely middle-aged. The species was fashionable from 1984 onwards although observed and commented on as early as 1928.

Young Hickory: James K. Polk (1795–1849), 11th US President (1845–9), because he had a similar background to – and attributes in common with – *Old Hickory*. Also: the **First Dark Horse**, because at the 1844 Convention, the Democrats eliminated Martin Van Buren unexpectedly and chose Polk.

Young Pretender, the: Prince Charles Edward (Louis Philip Casimir) Stuart (1722–88), also **the Young Chevalier**, elder son of James – *the Old Pretender* – claimant to the English throne who led the unsuccessful uprising in 1745. Charles advanced as far as Derby, but then his followers were dispersed and he escaped to France. He was a brave and romantic figure to the Highlanders when young – their **Bonnie Prince Charlie** – and was supported by the French until he became an embarrassment to their government. He wandered through Europe on behalf of a hopeless cause, lapsed into drunkenness and debauchery. Also affectionately known as **the Highland Laddie.**

Young Roscius, the: see *Roscius.*

Young Sinatra, the: see POP STARS.

Yvonne: see 'PRIVATE EYE' NICKNAMES.

Z

zany: an idiot, a preposterous fool, also a mimic because it was originally the theatrical name for a buffoon who mimicked the clown in Italian comedy (*commedia dell' arte*), the diminutive of the Italian Giovanni (John), and it was transferred as a nickname for anyone considered to be foolish or ridiculous. It was familiar as such in Shakespeare's day. Berowne uses it in *Love's Labour's Lost*, V:ii: 'Some carry-tale, some please-man, some slight zany.' This English adoption of the diminutive of Giovanni has been carried forward to our own Johnny for John, in such an expression as 'He's a silly Johnny'. Johnny has been used as a nickname in several ways, including that for a man-about-town: cf. the Edwardian *Stage Door Johnny*. Zany lingered in the vocabulary but was almost forgotten by the nineteenth century; and then the Americans retrieved it — as with so many old English words — and refurbished it. A favourite description of the Marx brothers' films was 'zany comedy': the word has come to mean outrageous foolery.

Zero Mostel: see FILM STARS.

Zoot Sims: see JAZZ MUSICIANS.

INDEX